CONTENTS

ILLUSTRATIONS

SAINT BENEDICT SCHOOL
DUFFIELD ROAD
DERBY DE22 1JD

GENERAL EDITOR'S INTRODUCTION

The history of charity-giving and charity legislation is very long, but also complicated and confusing. Anybody who, like me, is secretary of an organisation with charitable status will appreciate the problem – charity legislation, despite the many improvements of the past decade, is demanding and requires a good deal of paperwork for its administration. In the past this was perhaps less the case, but instead the uncertainties and doubts about charities and their status were legion. The result was an immense and well-nigh uncountable number of charities, quasi-charities, bogus charities and almost-charities, many of which have left records to tantalise and bewilder the local historian.

When conducting research into local history, and attempting to investigate such topics as the welfare of the poor or the religious attitudes of the community, it has never been easy to understand the implications of charitable status in the past, and to be able to see the context within which a local charity operated. Furthermore, the reasons for the decline of individual charities, or for changes in their role and status, have often been unclear.

In this book Norman Alvey has provided a summary of the progress of charity-giving, and the legislative framework of charities, from the early sixteenth century to the present day, tracing the way in which different rationales for charity have been reflected in official attitudes to the charities themselves, and showing how the vagueness and imprecision of the statute law meant that much was determined by an endless succession of individual cases.

In an important section he brings the story up to date, showing how the 1992 and 1993 Acts, and their immediate predecessors, have helped to clarify some of the key areas, and how the criteria for acceptance as a charity have evolved to the present. By emphasising the current position he makes a contrast with the uncertainties of the past. This book provides a clear and ordered introduction to this complex subject, and it will be warmly welcomed by local historians who seek to disentangle the intricacies of charities in their own area of research.

Alan Crosby

AUTHOR'S INTRODUCTION

This book deals with charity in England and Wales from Tudor times to the present day. Charities were intended to meet contemporary needs, and so some account of the contemporary political and social problems – the context of charity – is also given. Attitudes to philanthropy have varied over the last six hundred years and chapter headings indicate the prevailing stance during a particular period - though, of course, in each period not all benefactors reacted in the same way.

Some people supposed that the wide-ranging social legislation introduced after 1945 would provide for all welfare needs. The Nathan Committee,[59] set up in 1950 to investigate charities, considered that 'the basic question confronting the Committee was what remained for charities to do' – yet it concluded that ever greater demands were being made on them. Certainly, our charities still play an important role in this country and abroad.

In the past, benefactors liked to see their endowments set up as charitable trusts because they were attracted by the special privileges these trusts enjoyed – the right to exist in perpetuity and to have imperfectly worded deeds amended so that the donor's wishes were not frustrated. Legislation aimed to encourage such trusts and to see that their privileges were not abused.

Today many large charities have no permanent endowments but they do raise considerable annual incomes from subscriptions. For them the advantages of ancient privileges associated with endowment are outweighed by the fiscal concessions offered with subscriptions, and recent legislation has concentrated on monitoring the operations (particularly those for raising funds) of those institutions which gain these concessions. To qualify for these legal and fiscal perquisites it is necessary to become registered as a charity, yet the term *charity* has never been exhaustively defined in legislation. The concept has gradually evolved, partly from statutes, but largely from court decisions, a process outlined in the later chapters.

Norman Alvey

ACKNOWLEDGEMENTS

All those whom I consulted while garnering information have been most helpful, and I am particularly grateful to the Charity Commission Library, to the House of Lords Record Office and to those charities which have been generous with advice and illustrations. The clarity and layout of the text have been considerably improved by Alan Crosby, who also introduced me to several additional sources of information about charities. Kevin Fuller has generously advised on the meaning of legal terms and on the correct presentation of references to statutes and cases.

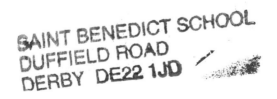
SAINT BENEDICT SCHOOL
DUFFIELD ROAD
DERBY DE22 1JD

CHAPTER 1

CHARITY FOR PERSONAL SALVATION

The medieval view

When *The Canterbury Tales* was written most charities were religious and Chaucer, a shrewd observer and one of the liveliest social commentators of all time, did not overlook them. The poor parson incurred the poet's approval as

> *He sette nat his benefice to hyre,*
> *And leet his sheep encombred in the myre,*
> *And ran to London, un-to seynt Poules*
> *To seken him a chaunterie for soules.*

To explain the function of such a chantry throws light upon the general attitude to charity at that time. It was believed that there were three states of after-life – heaven, hell and purgatory. Perfect souls went straight to heaven, the irredeemably wicked went to hell, and the remainder entered purgatory for a limited period of suffering to purge their sins. The duration of this period could be reduced, not only by the good deeds done during one's life but also by the prayers of others after one's death. Testators would leave money to pay priests to chant masses for their souls. Such bequests could be munificent, even directing that separate chapels were built for the chantry priests. The earliest chantry chapel recorded in England, that of Bishop Hugh of Wells in Lincoln Cathedral, was founded in 1235; many other chantries were set up after the Black Death of 1348-9. Prayers were said not only for the testator, but also for those who had gone before, and the poor were often remembered. In 1301, for example, Mary de Bassingbourn left money to maintain four canons to pray for her soul and for the souls of her two husbands and her parents, while she also provided for almshouses for seven poor and infirm men.

In this period, too, the poor performed a desirable function – they provided the better-off with opportunities for good deeds in life. Donors, more concerned with their own salvation than with the real needs of others, would therefore have been greatly alarmed if the poor had disappeared. No serious or concerted efforts were made to tackle poverty, but thousands of indiscriminate gifts were made instead – for example, doles of meat and drink, or the distribution of money and clothing at the funeral of the testator.

The poor included wandering beggars, but the settled poor – widows, low wage earners, the unemployed, the sick – were regarded in a more kindly light. But charitable donations could go elsewhere. Donors might be persuaded that fellows of colleges were poor and deserving of charity. Gifts were frequently left to the four orders of friars – the Dominicans, Franciscans, Augustinians and Carmelites. As Chaucer's friar explains

> *For unto a povre ordre for to yive*
> *Is signe that a man is wel y-shrive.*

Such personal pleas had powerful backing. The papacy urged testators to make gifts *ad pias causas*, and in the thirteenth century Pope Gregory IX threatened denial of the Eucharist and burial in unconsecrated ground to those who refused. People who died intestate were also in error so, to enhance their chances of salvation, the Church would obtain the right to administer such estates and distribute a portion for charitable purposes. Such bequests were often used to benefit monasteries, to support the clergy, or to improve and maintain the fabric of churches, but they were not confined to the

1. The Ramryge chantry chapel in the abbey church of St. Alban's. Thomas Ramryge was abbot from 1492 to 1521 and was succeeded by Cardinal Wolsey. The chapel was completed in about 1522 and was the last building work to be under taken at the abbey before the dissolution of the monasteries *(reproduced by kind permission of Dr. D.J. Kelsall).*

betterment of religious institutions alone. The Church was to incur much censure later but, in its prime, it paid for many public works and did much to relieve those in need. In Yorkshire, for example, chantry priests often acted as schoolmasters, as at Tickhill, and monastic foundations in that county distributed the very considerable sum of over £300 annually for the relief of poverty. In Norwich the St Giles Hospital, founded by the bishop in 1249, provided meals and beds for poor, aged and infirm persons and was so well regarded that it continued to attract support even under the Tudors.

The *cy-pres* doctrine

The Franciscan Order was forbidden to hold property of its own, so trusts were set up to hold assets on its behalf. It became usual for such institutions and causes to be administered as charitable trusts, which attracted important privileges. The law limiting the duration of trusts could be waived if they were charitable, and donors could be assured that their gifts would remain effective for all time. Furthermore, the terms of ordinary trust deeds became 'void for uncertainty' if they were imprecisely worded.

However, if a general charitable intention was obvious, the courts had power to infer what the donor's wishes might have been and to modify the deed accordingly. Thus donors would not have their intentions frustrated by some legal technicality. This concession, allowing the amendment of a charitable trust deed, became known as the *cy-pres doctrine*. It is not clear whether the term *cy-pres* derived from the medieval French *ici pres* [near this] or from *aussi pres* [as near as possible] but the ecclesiastical courts preferred the laxer interpretation. It was, and indeed is, a principle of the greatest importance and is referred to frequently throughout this book. The *cy-pres* doctrine was also applied if the objects of a charitable trust proved impossible to implement or if they became outmoded.

Since the time of Justinian the church had claimed the right to supervise legacies devoted to pious uses, and during the thirteenth century in England the ecclesiastical courts assumed jurisdiction over all charitable bequests in this country. They exercised considerable freedom when inferring the donor's wishes under the *cy-pres* doctrine. To them the main object of such gifts was the spiritual welfare of donors, which would be impaired if trusts were declared void, and so the loose interpretation of the doctrine was favoured – it allowed considerable freedom to turn the imperfect wording to the advantage of both church and donor. Later, however, the stricter alternative was used.

Charity and the late medieval church

As early as the fourteenth century the prestige of the church was on the wane. This was partly due to the worldliness of its representatives, typified by Chaucer's Monk, 'a lord ful fat and in good point', who had found the simple rule of St Benedict too strict for his liking and unashamedly enjoyed the pleasures of the table and the chase. In addition, however, there was the vexed question of the use of tithe revenues. Although it had been customary for a portion of such revenues to be allocated to the poor, many monastic foundations, when they appropriated the tithes on their vast estates, did not accept this obligation in full.

Only a very small percentage was ever recovered for alms, despite various decrees which sought to enforce the custom. Under Richard II[2] it was recognised that appropriations of benefices, and hence of tithes, harmed parishioners' interests, and it was laid down not only that all licences for such appropriations should be made in Chancery, but also that these should provide adequate endowments for vicars and for sums to be distributed for 'povres parochiens des...esglises en eide de lair vivre & sustenance a toutz jours' [for poor parishioners of the churches to help their life and sustenance at all times].

Henry IV tried to reinforce this obligation,[3] but further action had to be taken in 1414. An Act of Henry V[4] complained that, though donors had been very generous, the hospitals they had founded 'be now for the most Part decayed and the Goods and Profits of the same, by divers Persons, as well Spiritual as Temporal, withdrawn and spent in other Use, whereby many Men and Women have died in great Misery for

Default of Aid, Living and Succour to the Displeasure of God, and Peril to the Souls of such Manner of Spenders'. It was ordered that they should be inspected and reformed where necessary.

Again, the Church was in a position to influence the expansion of education, but did not always use this power beneficially or positively. In the capital, for example, the approval of the bishop of London and the chancellor of St Paul's was necessary to establish a school. Three church schools, originating in the twelfth century (St Paul's, St Martin-le-Grand and St Mary-le-Bow) had been vigorous and flourishing but each had fallen into decay before the end of the fifteenth century. Despite influential, even royal, protests the ecclesiastics were able to maintain their monopoly and many attempts to found private schools in London were quashed. At York, the monopoly of St Peter's school was maintained by the cathedral chapter which prohibited, in 1426 and again in 1486, the opening of any other school within a radius of ten miles of the city. In Norfolk, grammar school education was seldom, if ever, available outside monastery walls.

This ecclesiastical obstruction stimulated the setting up of many modest endowments for secular purposes. Initially these, too, were handled by ecclesiastical courts, but there was increasing irritation over the fees which such courts charged, and it was suspected that their officers were corrupt – not surprisingly, if Chaucer's *Somnour* was a typical example. He, of the 'fyr-reed cherubinnes face' and 'lecherous, as a sparwe' was prepared to wink at other men's sins if well paid for it. In fact, litigants were becoming increasingly disenchanted with all existing courts of law.

The handling of charity law by secular courts

By the fourteenth century royal justice was mainly administered by the courts of common law, 'common' because it was supposed to apply to all the king's subjects throughout his realm. There were three courts, those of Common Pleas, the King's Bench and the Exchequer of Pleas, and it was not unknown for them to give conflicting judgments. They were cumbersome, with complex rules based on hoary precedent and, as they refused to try more than one issue at a time, delays were prolonged. The system became further debased during the political chaos of the fifteenth century, when local lords were able to intimidate juries and defy the law. Disappointed litigants turned to the king for fair and common sense solutions to their problems. He referred their petitions to his chancellor, who was not so bound by precedent, and by the early sixteenth century the chancellor was giving decisions in his own name.

This Court of Chancery dealt not with crime, but with issues raised by private individuals protecting their own interests. No oral evidence was taken when trying these *suits* (not *actions*), and *decrees* (not *judgments*) were issued. The court tried to act according to the spirit rather than the letter of the law, and might apply statutes to cases for which no specific provision had been made. This recourse to the general principles of justice became known as *equity*. The Court of Chancery was relatively cheap, efficient and just. During the fifteenth and sixteenth centuries its jurisdiction expanded rapidly. This included acquiring the responsibility for charitable trusts, although the transfer of this function from the ecclesiastical courts was probably inevitable as, since the time of Henry VI, there had been a great shift from religious to secular trusts.

Judgments formed under *equity* prevailed if they conflicted with those made in the courts of common law. Not unnaturally, those administering the common law objected strongly and there was considerable controversy throughout the sixteenth century. In 1598 a ruling prohibited chancery from re-examining matters which had already been determined in the common law courts, as it was felt that otherwise 'suits would be infinite and no one could be in peace for anything that the law had given him by judgment'.

Nevertheless Lord Chancellor Ellesmere continued to intervene, which provoked a monumental clash with Lord Coke, Chief Justice of Common Pleas. From this Ellesmere emerged victorious: a royal decree of 18 July 1616 conferred on the chancellor power to review all matters at common law both before and after judgment. This may have been because James I, who saw himself as a latter-day Solomon, was more sympathetic to those courts (prerogative and chancery) where he felt he had more influence.[60] The rules of equity have prevailed ever since. When, for example, St John's College, Cambridge, petitioned the lord chancellor to compel Robert Platt to convey land left to the college by his father, the conveyance was enforced in 1657 under equity, even though the gift was held to be void under common law due to the use of incorrect procedures.

The decline in the religious charities after the Reformation

The decline in religious trusts accelerated under Henry VIII. Considerable restraint on their creation was imposed by an Act passed in 1532,[5] which also dissuaded donors from transferring land to chantries. In 1545 another Act[9] made all such endowments – which were considerable – forfeit to the Crown. This had not been hard to justify, at least as far as its instigators were concerned, as funds for many chantries had already been appropriated by the priest or by the founder's heirs. The 1545 legislation was restated and reinforced under Edward VI in an Act[10] which differentiated between 'charitable' and 'superstitious' uses. It criticised those who 'by devising and phantasinge vayne opynions of Purgatorye and Masses satisfactorye to be done for them which be departed, the which doctryne and vayn opynion by nothing more in Mayntance and upholde than by the abuse of Trentalle [set of 30 requiem masses] Chauntries and other provisions made for the contynuance of the said blyndness and ignoraunce'. It held, too, 'that a greate p[ar]te of Superstition and Errors in Christian Religion hath byn brought into the mynde and estimacon of men' and that chantry revenues would be better spent on education and other charitable objectives.

This, and other timeworn approaches to saving one's soul, were eventually outlawed by the Act of Uniformity of 1558,[12] passed in the year that Elizabeth came to the throne. This deplored the repeal by Mary Tudor of Edward's Act which had set up 'one uniforme Order of Common Service and Prayour', saying that the repeal was 'to the greate Decay of the due Honour of God'. The Act of Uniformity set out severe penalties for those who neglected or refused to use the Book of Common Prayer. The definition and treatment of 'superstitious uses' was, however, to cause difficulty for many years to come. Even the appointment of chaplains was queried, and in 1606 the chancellor and the justices of the King's Bench had to rule that finding *cuidam Capellano ad Divina Celebranda*, in a certain church or chapel, is no superstitious use within the statute of 1 Edward VI...and the reason is, because it is the general case of all parsons in England'.

Gifts 'for popish purposes' were, predictably, forfeit to the Crown, so secret trusts were frequently set up by wealthy sympathisers with the Roman Catholic cause. If exposed, these trusts were of course declared void, and their assets redistributed. Although James I made no claim on two secret trusts, one set up to relieve poor recusants[61] and the other for Jesuits and seminary priests, Lord Chancellor Ellesmere, with the concurrence of the chief justices, held the trusts to be 'unlawful and merely void' and the assets went to the heirs, Protestants in both cases.

During the seventeenth century several decisions were taken which helped to formulate the concept of 'prerogative' (as opposed to judicial) *cy-pres*. By this means property left for the support of an illegal charity would be diverted to an alternative use, not by the courts but by the Crown. Here, an important decision was taken concerning a group of Puritan churchmen, who had collected over £6,300 to fill livings with men of their own choice and religious persuasion. Archbishop Laud and Charles I took steps to suppress the movement, and in 1633 the attorney-general argued in the equity side of the Exchequer that the group had incorporated themselves unlawfully and were attempting to encourage schism. The group rebutted this, saying that they had not acted as a corporation and that the services and preaching would have been Anglican. The court decided against the group and the Crown was able to manage the fund for purposes of its own choosing.[62] After this it became common practice for the Crown to apply property devoted to the use of a 'false' religion to other charitable purposes. This roused much debate, especially in the late 1680s when James II enforced such trusts for their original Roman Catholic purposes.

Mortmain and the resulting restrictions on charities

The Court of Chancery had preserved the existing privileges of charitable trusts, including the application of the *cy-pres* doctrine. In 1657, for example, the chancellor, Lord Verulam, (formerly Sir Francis Bacon) ruled that £1,000 left to maintain two fellows and six scholars at Emmanuel College, Cambridge could all be used for scholars, as the maintenance payments allotted for fellows were inadequate.[63] Bacon is reported to have said

'That he did not intend to alter anything concerning the disposition of the legacy contrary to the will, except it were in that which was impossible to be performed, which might prove a hindrance and inconvenience to the college; and also that, in that which was necessary to be altered in respect of impossibility and inconvenience as aforesaid, he desired to tie himself as near as might be to the will and meaning of the testator in the ordering and disposing there of'

This decision was controversial, as not everyone considered that it would have been 'impossible' to carry out the testator's wishes.

Chancery differed from the ecclesiastical courts in one important respect – it discouraged gifts of land to charities. A charitable trust is never under age, never dies, never commits felonies and never marries. Once it holds property that property could effectively be removed from the land market and – in the medieval period – from the feudal system. The transfer [alienation] of land into the 'dead hand' (or *mortmain*) of charity terminated payments of many feudal dues, and the augmentation of vast monatic estates by bequests of land had particularly dismayed feudal lords, including the king. Properly, licences were required from all feudal lords, from the immediate lord right up to the king, before land could be 'alienated into mortmain' but, eventually, only licence from the king was necessary.

Religious houses avoided this requirement by such devices as renting land on very long leases or taking the profits from land which they did not apparently own. Between the thirteenth and sixteenth centuries a considerable body of legislation was devoted to plugging loopholes in the law of mortmain.[1] Despite this, during the reign of Henry VIII a pamphleteer was able to claim that ecclesiastics 'have begged so importunately that they have gotten into their hands more than a third part of all your Realm'. After the Reformation, although the alienation of land to religious houses had ceased, there was a continuing fear that the process might be perpetuated by the accumulation of charity lands, and therefore the official view was that bequests of land on any scale were undesirable – the endowments of charities should, if possible, take other forms.

Charity and social welfare

At the same time as charitable funds from religious sources diminished, a decrease accelerated by the dissolution of the monasteries, the charitable needs of society as a whole were increasing. There was widespread concern, in the late fifteenth and early sixteenth centuries, about social upheaval and turmoil. The feudal system of land tenure was breaking down and many, losing the land on which they had subsisted, became destitute. Sir Thomas More complained that 'noblemen and gentlemen, yea and certain abbots, holy men no doubt, not contenting themselves with the yearly revenues and profits that were wont to grow to their forefathers...leave no ground for tillage...and enclose many thousand acres of ground together within one pale or hedge, the husbandmen be thrust out of their own, or else by covin or fraud or by violent oppression they be put beside it, or by wrongs and injuries they be so wearied that they be compelled to sell all...And when they have wandered abroad till that be spent, what can they else do but steal, and then justly pardy be hanged, or else go about a-begging?'.[64]

In addition to this problem there were major demographic changes as towns grew and as new prosperity began to affect regions such as the north-west. Difficulties were further increased when the nobility, under pressure from Henry VII, turned from factional strife to the peaceful management of their estates and in doing so discarded their quasi-military retainers. These 'swashbuckling ruffians' added a dangerous element to the army of the unemployed. Finally, and crucially, the dissolution of the monasteries itself threw many of the lay servants of religious houses onto the labour market. Great numbers of rogues and vagabonds, existing on alms supplemented by begging and petty crime, plagued the country and stern laws were enacted to suppress them.

Because a proportion of the parochial tithes was supposed to be reserved for the poor, the parishes were expected to deal with these problems. Vagrants were returned to their home parishes for the receipt of poor relief – or for punishment – and this practice was reinforced when successive Tudor governments made the parish the secular unit of administration. Initially all poor people were considered to be responsible for their own misfortunes, and 'strong valiaunt beggars' were not distinguished from 'olde sick lame feble and impotent persones not able to labour for ther livyng'. In 1535, however, an Act[8] was passed which allowed licensed beggars to operate, although only in their own parish.

The regulation of poverty in the late sixteenth century

Hitherto alms had usually been given on a somewhat indiscriminate or unspecific basis, such as the bequest of £42 by the Earl of Northumberland in 1489 to provide gowns for the poor, or that of £100 by Sir William Paston, a Norfolk landowner who died in 1524, for doles of meat, drink and money. By the mid-sixteenth century the official attitude was that such handouts, and others even more casual, encouraged begging and 'dependency', and attempts were therefore made to organise relief for the poor on a more orderly basis. Under Edward VI an Act was passed 'To thintent that valyaunt Beggars ydle and loytering parsones must be avoyded and the impotent feble

2. Sir Thomas More, chancellor of England from 1529 to 1532 *(The Royal Collection 1994, Her Majesty the Queen.)*

and lame provyded for, which ar poore in verie dede'.[11] In the corporate boroughs, every year during Whit Week, the mayor, assisted by others, should appoint 'twoo hable parsons or moo' to collect voluntary contributions to be distributed as alms to the poor each week. Those who could do some work were to get less than those who had no means of livelihood 'but none to goo or sitt openlie a begging'.

In 1594, after a succession of poor harvests and during a severe economic depression, the government was forced to acknowledge the existence of a third class of poor people, neither impotent nor vagrant but genuinely unemployed. It had finally been realised that there were 'labouring persons not able to live off their labour', but the legal definitions of this state were vague, and it was left to the local authorities to distinguish the culpable from the unfortunate. Vagrants, defined in 1572 as able bodied men without land or master who declined to accept employment,[13] were still treated harshly, but justices were required to compile registers of the 'true' poor and to arrange for their relief in their home parish.

London had sanctioned a compulsory poor rate as early as 1547 and Norwich, Bristol, York and other towns were soon to follow. This was imposed nationally by an act of 1597 (reinforced and codified under the 'Old Poor Law' of 1601),[15] and justices had the power to jail those who refused to pay. Overseers of the poor were to serve, unpaid, to assist constables and churchwardens in the collection and distribution of the poor rate. It was clearly established that responsibility for the poor lay with the parish (or, in the north of England, the township) and was in secular, not church, hands. Statutory and charitable relief were now intended to further civil, not ecclesiastical, ends.

As the Nathan Committee saw it, 'to the middle ages the problem seemed centred in cleansing the souls of the faithful from the sin of avarice. Almsgiving was thus more a means to the salvation of the soul of the benefactor than an endeavour to diagnose and alleviate the needs of the beneficiary'.[59] This attitude was to change.

CHAPTER 2

CHARITY AS A SOCIAL RESPONSIBILITY

Encouragement of secular charity

Tudor governments did not expect the statutory system of poor relief to be sufficient on its own. On the contrary, they looked to voluntary effort to produce most of the funds. Voluntary provision in the field of social welfare was already considerable. There were new secular trusts, some administered by guilds, including permanent incorporated associations such as hospitals and the colleges of Oxford and Cambridge. There were also innumerable local initiatives, often on a very small scale and with very modest and geographically-restricted roles. Examples are extremely numerous, and often seem to us rather eccentric. For example, there were the cow charities, common in Cheshire, which rented out cows at very low rates to 'poor and godly parishioners'.

At Alresford in Essex the morning milk from two cows was given to the poor between Whitsun to Michaelmas. A three-acre field in West Retford, Nottinghamshire, was let rent-free to a person willing to maintain a bull for the use of parishioners. Other bequests were more substantial. In 1493, for example, John Bedford of Aylesbury bequeathed a number of houses and 107 acres of land to the parish of Aylesbury on trust, intended for the perpetual care of the roads and to provide alms for the poor. John Downman, son of the lord of the manor of Pocklington in Yorkshire, conveyed property worth £267 in 1514 to set up a school. For the pupils he endowed five scholarships at St John's College, Cambridge, and in 1551 his foundation was transferred by Act of Parliament to the college and the archbishop of York with power to appoint the headmaster. In 1566 Sir Richard Fulmerston of Thetford, Norfolk, left £160 to found a free grammar school for thirty boys and a hospital for four elderly and deserving persons. All Tudor administrations considered that such activities should be encouraged, and an Act was passed in 1572 to assist those who wished to found hospitals and almshouses.[14] Under a further Act of 1597 it was no longer necessary to obtain a licence from the queen before erecting hospitals or abiding and working houses for the poor, and this could now be effected by 'deede inrolled in the High Court of Chancery'.[16]

The regulation of charities from 1601

While favouring genuine donors the government was determined that charity privileges should not be abused. The 1535 Statute of Uses[7] awarded the legal title of an estate to the person who had the use of it. Thus, owners who had tried to take advantage of charitable status while in reality retaining personal control of their assets found that they could no longer claim the protection of the Court of Chancery, but became subject to the courts of common law. To claim such protection, ownership and use had to be vested in a charitable trust.

It was also clearly intended that trust funds should be properly managed, and not misused. In 1597 an 'Act to reforme Deceits and Breaching of Trust, touching lands given to Charitable Uses'[17] was passed. This was refined and amplified in 1601 by an 'Act to redress the Misemployment of Lands, Goods and Stocks of Money heretofore given to Charitable Uses'. This second Act was commonly known as the *Statute of Charitable Uses*,[18] and its interpretational element has remained fundamental to charity law ever since, even though it is now repealed. In a practical way it authorised the chancellor to set up commissions in each county, consisting of the 'Byshop of everie severall Diocesse

15

and his Chanceller [and] other persons of good and sounde behaviour' to enquire into 'Abuses Breaches of Trustes Negligences Mysimploimentes' by trustees. Parishioners were encouraged to bring allegations of breaches of trust before the county commission. Interested parties, aggrieved by the commissioners' decrees, could make a final appeal to the chancellor.

The commissioners were empowered to regulate the use of charitable funds to ensure that the founder's wishes were carried out; to set up stocks of materials to provide work for the unemployed; to determine the amounts to be paid to poor maids about to be married; to supply and cure defects in conveyances of property left to charities; and to uphold gifts to charity where the trust deed was imperfectly worded.

They were soon busy. In 1616, for example, churchwardens and others from every Nottinghamshire parish were summoned to give evidence, and the probate registers were searched for wills containing charitable bequests. It was found that rents for the use of the poor had been pocketed by local landowners, while other charities had been 'lost'. In Bedfordshire and some other counties charity money was being used to reduce the poor rate, or was diverted to other purposes. At Bishops Stortford the commissioners were not satisfied that funds for the grammar school and other charities were being properly applied. Later, in 1716, the High Court of Chancery ordered 'that the Churchwardens and Overseers of the Poor of the said parish do continue respectively to reserve the Rents and Profits of the respective Charity Estates according to the Decree of the Commissioners but the Churchwardens are not to issue any of the Charity moneys to make any ornaments of the Church without the Consent of the major part of the four trustees first had in writing'.

The preamble to the Act of 1601 lists charitable uses, but religion is not specifically mentioned. Charity had moved from being a spiritual matter, of concern to the religious, to being an instrument of social policy. The Elizabethan legislation remained in force even during the Commonwealth, though the civil war left it without the support of strong parish government and the commissioners became dilatory and their procedures expensive. After the Restoration most litigants reverted to the old practice of acting through the attorney general, the representative of the Crown which, as *parens patriae*, had the right to oversee charities. Some statistics may illustrate the decline in the use of commissions. Over 950 such investigations were set up between 1660 and 1742, but only six were created from 1743 to 1818.

The financing of charity

Not long before his death Henry VIII gave the convent of Grey Friars (to become Christ's Hospital) and the hospital of St Bartholomew for the relief of the poor. Edward VI transferred endowments of over £15,000 to the Corporation of London to maintain the five 'royal' hospitals (St Thomas', St Bartholomew's, Christ's, Bethlehem and Bridewell). Elizabeth's Act of 1572[14] for the relief of the poor in hospitals recalled this earlier royal generosity and, expecting the royal example to be followed by others, added that 'it is hoped many more hereafter will likewise charitably give'. Such reliance on voluntary charity was justified: the statute of 1601 was introduced not to restore or to introduce the idea of giving for charitable purposes, but to provide safeguards for a system which was already expanding rapidly. A crucial role was played by the business community, carefully cultivated by Elizabeth, and the more prudent of her predecessors, who needed its support for political and financial reasons. After the dissolution of the monasteries, much of the wealth of religious houses found its way into private hands. The merchants and the newly-enriched gentry made large

3. The Convent of Grey Friars near Newgate, granted to the City of London by King Henry VIII in 1546. It was to become Christ's Hospital (*reproduced by kind permission of Noel Osborne, Phillimore & Co.*).

contributions to a wide range of charities, particularly in their own localities. Jordan estimated that in the early sixteenth century the merchants of the City of London contributed over half of the money raised for charitable purposes. This did not only affect London itself, for many men from the provinces who 'made good' in London commercial circles endowed charities in their birthplaces or native towns.

This type of philanthropy was not entirely disinterested, especially in the case of London merchants, for it was claimed that there were 'greate nombers of poor lame ydell amd maysterless men dispersed in dyvers parts of this Realme, but chiefly aboute this Cittie of London', and this was perceived as a serious threat which donors hoped to mitigate by relieving distress. Perhaps it was also sensed that, with suitable instruction, some of the idle poor could become assets to the community.

The endowment of schools

By the second half of the seventeenth century educational opportunities were probably more widespread than at any time for the next two hundred years. Until the Reformation education was largely under Church control, and often available only for the clergy and those associated with them. After the 1540s, however, many secular schools were founded. In London, Merchant Taylors' School, supported mainly by the liveried company, was founded in 1560. Queen Elizabeth assured revenues to support 120 boys at Westminster School, and by 1660 about £13,970 had been donated by Londoners to support education at Christ's Hospital (including a small sum of £160 for educating girls). At that time the recognised London schools had a total enrolment of about 1,500. The period 1571-1660 was a golden age for the founding of grammar schools throughout the country, although in some areas such activity did not reach its peak until the end of this time.

In Lancashire church and lay authorities were lamenting the lack of instruction for the young before 1515, but in that year Hugh Oldham founded the Manchester Grammar School: a master and usher were appointed and expected to speak Latin within the school. Scholars were charged one penny on admission, in order to pay two of the poor scholars to clean the buildings once a week, and diseased or disabled pupils were not admitted. The school hours were from 7 a.m. to 6 p.m., except for those who had to travel long distances, and no cockfights or unlawful games were allowed. After 1515 comparable, though more modest, schools were founded in many Lancashire towns and villages, a movement perhaps inspired in part by examples such as Manchester Grammar School.

Sir John Port of Etwall in Derbyshire, by his will of 9 March 1556, left funds to provide an almshouse at Etwall itself and for a school at Repton. By 1622 the schoolmaster at Repton was paid £40 a year and the usher who taught grammar, £20. Each was provided with a house and garden – though the usher who taught writing, ciphering and book-keeping was paid £15 and had to make do with lodgings. Sons of all persons living in Etwall or Repton were admitted free, and four poor foundationers were paid £5 to help with the teaching. By 1836 Repton school had eight foundationers and fourteen free scholars; between forty and fifty fee-paying pupils boarded with the schoolmaster or an Usher, and four or five were day pupils. All were taught together, without distinction, and they studied the classics, writing, accounts, mathematics, history and geography.

The surviving medieval church schools could not easily compete with these richly endowed secular foundations. There were occasional exceptions; for example, John Colet, appointed dean of St Paul's in 1505, using the large fortune inherited from his father and with help from his father's company, the Mercers, rejuvenated St Paul's School and between 1508 and 1512 accommodation was provided for 153 students.

Charities and apprenticeships

Training was not neglected and considerable sums were left to support apprenticeships – for example, Cogan's Charity at Hull (1753), which gave its girl apprentices £6 marriage portions provided that they had completed 'six years in respectable servitude'. An Act of 1610[19] which attempted to regulate the provision of apprenticeships stated that much money had been given for this purpose and, unless the donor had specified otherwise, the funds should be disbursed by the local corporation or the parson assisted by the constable, the churchwardens and the overseers of the poor.

Justices of the peace would supervise the distribution, and if there was neglect fines could be levied, of which half was to go to poor relief. Masters of apprentices were to undertake to use the income only and to return the fee at the end of the apprenticeship, thus giving a revolving fund. Their apprenticeship completed, young men could obtain loans to help them set up in business. These loans might be interest-free, as with the charity of Sir Thomas White who left gifts to twenty-four towns, including Coventry, Northampton, Leicester, Nottingham and Warwick. Alternatively, low rates of interest might be charged, as when the sixth earl of Shrewsbury left substantial funds to Sheffield, Rotherham and Pontefract. Income from such interest would, in its turn, be distributed to the poor.

The support of charity by the wealthy

The philosophy that 'blessed are the poor' was proclaimed in the Sermon on the Mount, and for some the very act of giving was its own reward. Others became more discriminating, particularly after statutory provisions for basic needs had been introduced. During the late fifteenth and early sixteenth centuries benefactions were mostly of alms for immediate use, but from 1520 onwards there was a rapid increase in the number of endowments which were in the form of legally constituted charitable trusts with specified objects. It has been estimated that between 1550 and 1650 private endowments were providing twice as much annually as the poor rate, and the overall annual income rose tenfold (fourfold if inflation is taken into account). Although income from the poor rate matched that from charitable endowments by 1650, and surpassed it by 1700, the rich were apparently accepting their social responsibilities, and the failure of a wealthy testator to settle a substantial gift on charity was considered shocking.

Such gifts could be munificent. Thomas Guy, a successful bookseller who accumulated a vast fortune from shrewd investments, which included selling his South Sea stock before the bubble burst, paid for three new wards at St Thomas's Hospital in 1707 and founded Guy's Hospital in 1722. Though this followed the traditional cloistered layout of the old monastic infirmaries, it was the first secular, purpose-built hospital in the country. When Guy died in 1724 he left it the residue of his estate, amounting to some £240,000. Support for such generosity was by no means universal, and there was an outcry that the legal heirs were being sacrificed to a rich man's vanity.

This seems unfair since, although a bachelor, he had provided liberally for his family. It was alleged that he underpaid and overworked his staff and he certainly spent little on himself, dining off an old newspaper on his shop counter and 'being as little nice in regard to his apparel'. He may have offended the establishment by refusing the office of sheriff of London, with its attendant expenses, but he had always contributed generously to charity and many of his benefactions remained concealed until after his death. Nevertheless while the motives of Thomas Guy may have been entirely laudable and fair, there were other cases where heirs were being fraudulently deprived of their inheritance and these aroused genuine concern.

Charities, probate and inheritance

Before the reign of Charles II there had been much disquiet over nuncupative wills, those which the testator was supposed to have made orally. Such wills, which could include gifts to charity, had been upheld at law, but in 1677 an 'Act for the Prevention of fraudulent Practices in setting up Nuncupative Wills, which have been the Occasion of much Perjury' (the so-called 'Statute of Frauds')[20] was passed. This ruled that wills had to be in writing and proved by the oaths of at least three reliable witnesses. A nuncupative will was still valid for small estates worth £30 or less but the next of kin were given fourteen days in which to protest against its terms. The Statute of Frauds was reinforced by the Wills Act of 1837,[29] which also stipulated that witnesses could not benefit and that a will could be revoked only by another properly executed will or codicil in writing, or by marriage.

In the time of Henry VIII the 'Act concerning Uses and Wills'[7] painted a vivid picture of 'Persons as be visited with Sickness, in their extreme Agonies and Pains...being provoked by greedy and covetous Persons lying in wait about them, do many Times dispose indiscreetly and unadvisedly their Lands and Inheritances'. Perhaps one motive

4.   Thomas Guy (*c*1644-1724), engraving after a portrait by Vanderbank
(reproduced by kind permission of Guy's Gazette).

behind the 'Statute of Frauds' was a concern that testators might be terrified into making deathbed grants to religious charities, and there were apprehensive recollections of the vast accumulation of monastic estates during the Middle Ages. In the eighteenth century there was a similar mistrust of large charitable corporations, notably Queen Anne's Bounty, founded by the Queen in 1704 using the papal annates (originally imposed to fund the Crusades) which had been transferred to the Crown after the Reformation.[6]

It was intended to supplement the income of those Anglican priests impoverished after the passage of the Toleration Act in 1689.[21] Queen Anne's Bounty survived as a separate institution until 1948, when it was united with the Ecclesiastical Commission to form the Church Commission. Its constitution allowed it to receive any amount of property, regardless of the statutes of mortmain. The very considerable unpopularity of the Church of England during the mid-eighteenth century was, in part, the result of such large-scale accumulation of land.

5. The main entrance to Guy's Hospital, with the statue of Thomas Guy in the foreground *(reproduced by kind permission of Guy's Gazette).*

It was not only religious charities which fell out of favour in the early eighteenth century. A number of influential lawyers considered that all charities had been treated too leniently during the previous two hundred years, and though they were not prepared to override a century or more of case law they did feel that heirs were getting a raw deal. They questioned whether charities should be allowed to benefit from increases in the value of the original gifts and considered that, where the cy-pres doctrine had been loosely applied, there was a risk that heirs might be disinherited for the benefit of charities which the testator may not have intended to support. Lord Harcourt, in 1721, liked charity well but he would 'not steal leather to make poor mens shoes' and in 1736 Lord Hardwick appraised a judge's role as 'to do justice to all, and not to oppress any man for the sake of charity'. During this period, if a trust deed was amended any changed purpose had to correspond very closely to the stated wishes of the testator.

Disapproval among the judiciary of the accumulation of land by charitable corporations was made very clear in the preamble to the Mortmain Act of 1736:[22] 'Whereas Gifts or Alienations of Lands, Tenements or Hereditaments, in Mortmain, are prohibited or restrained by Magna Carta, and divers other wholsome Laws, as prejudicial to and against the common Utility; nevertheless this public Mischief has of late greatly increased by many large and improvident Alienations or Dispositions made by languishing or dying Persons, or by other Persons, to Uses called Charitable Uses, to take place after their Deaths, to the Disherison of their Heirs'.

The Act went on to discourage such practices by ruling that any deed leaving land (or money for the purchase of land) for charitable purposes had to be executed in the presence of two or more witnesses well before the testator died. Transfers of land had to be made at least twelve months, and of stock at least six months, before death; also, once made, such gifts were irrevocable. There had been vigorous protests during the

6. Captain Thomas Coram (*c*1688-1751), by William Hogarth *(reproduced by kind permission of the Thomas Coram Foundation for Children).*

passage of the bill and, although the universities and colleges of Oxford and Cambridge and Eton, Winchester and Westminster schools were exempted, other charities (including ecclesiastical charities) were not. The act was strictly applied yet it had less effect than was expected. Testators acted with surprising liberality during their own lifetimes; there were also generous gifts unconnected with land.

Charity and schools in the eighteenth century

There was in fact considerable charitable activity during the eighteenth century, not only by wealthy individuals but also by the 'middling class'. Money was raised from many small subscriptions, including those from congregations exhorted to give by charity sermons. Such 'charities', having no endowments and not being charitable trusts, attracted no special privileges and were not subject to charity legislation. Charity schools provided successful examples of this type of charity. In this area the Society for Propagating Christian Knowledge (S.P.C.K.), founded in 1699, played a leading role. It established its first school in the May of that year at St George's, Southwark, and by 1729 there were 132 schools with 5,225 pupils dispersed throughout the country. In 1782, about 12,000 attended the annual gathering of London charity school children at St Paul's. The S.P.C.K. strove to bring schooling to children of all denominations, but High Church Anglicans mounted strong opposition which the S.P.C.K. found it hard to combat. This alienated dissenters, who formed their own schools. Eventually the S.P.C.K. moved into the less tendentious areas of missionary work and publishing.

Usually the children were aged between seven and twelve, and some admitted children of the 'respectable' poor only. Others gave priority to the poorest and most 'vicious' children, turning away those 'who were not real objects of charity' and some of these resorted to boarding their pupils to prevent school discipline being undermined at home. In London funds and teachers were both readily available and pupils were easily absorbed into the London labour market, but elsewhere the charity school movement ran into difficulties.

In some places schools for the education of poor children had endowments and were run as legally constituted charitable trusts, but they had similar aims to the charity schools. Indeed the S.P.C.K. considered that the two types of school were complementary, and it did not encourage the establishment of subscription schools in areas where endowed schools already existed. All pupils were to have access to the bible, the catechism and the prayer book so it was essential that they learned to read, but it was considered less important that they should be able to write. Arithmetic might be taught at a later stage but only to boys. It was intended that pupils should emerge as industrious, sober and docile 'hewers of wood and drawers of water', and the uniforms were intentionally dull to discourage vanity. Girls were made fit for domestic service and boys trained to become good and honest apprentices in humble occupations. School governors made considerable efforts to shield pupils from the severities of the poor law – for example, by raising the money for apprenticeship fees.

Other institutions for destitute children appeared in the eighteenth century, one of the best known being the Foundling Hospital founded by Captain Thomas Coram in London in 1739. Nowadays it is, perhaps, possible to segregate oneself from misery but in the early eighteenth century the good captain was appalled to see babies abandoned on the dung heaps he was obliged to pass each day. Despite claims that his proposals would encourage wantonness and vice, and coarse insinuations about his own morals, he was at last able to muster powerful support and by 1756 the hospital had admitted 1,384 children. Today the Thomas Coram Foundation for Children has no institutional buildings but concentrates on helping its charges to be adopted or brought up by their own mothers.

Charity and care for the sick

Care for the sick also featured prominently during the eighteenth century. The medieval concept of a hospital as a refuge for the poor, the infirm and travellers had

7.   Dr. Andrew Reed (1787–1842), by George Patten. A Congregational minister, he founded three schools and two hospitals between 1813 and 1854 *(reproduced by kind permission of Reed's School)*.

been changing since Tudor times, and it was now recognised as an institution reserved for the sick. In addition to Guy's, four new general hospitals were founded in London during the first half of the eighteenth century: the Westminster in 1719, St George's in 1733, London in 1740 and Middlesex in 1745. All four, and many provincial hospitals, drew support from subscriptions or lump payments from governors which might account for between one half and one third of total income. Governors were entitled to vote on how the hospital was managed and to recommend patients for admission, the number of recommendations sometimes depending on the amount of money subscribed.

The endowed hospitals (St Thomas's, St Bartholomew's and Guy's) were relatively affluent and treated about three times as many patients as all the voluntary hospitals put together. Many of the latter, in contrast, ran short of money in the second half of the eighteenth century and fell into a shocking condition. It is thought that some charitable donors may have preferred, instead, to support maternity hospitals, of which several were founded in this period. St Luke's Hospital for Lunatics was opened in 1751 but the next new general hospital in London, the Charing Cross Hospital, was not established until 1818. Treatment was supposed to be free at endowed and voluntary hospitals alike, but fees were collected by nurses, porters and others. There were also burial deposits which patients could reclaim - provided they left the hospital alive. Partly as a protest against such charges Dr Marsden founded the Royal *Free* Hospital in 1828, and this also dispensed with governors' letters of recommendation.

During the eighteenth century hospitals were set up in many provincial centres. At York, for example, the County Hospital was founded in 1740, the Bootham Park Asylum started to care for lunatics during the 1770s, and in 1796 it was followed by the Quaker Retreat (which became a leader and pioneer in the humane treatment of the insane). At Cambridge, as early as 1719, Dr John Addenbrooke willed property for setting up a hospital, appointing one of his executors and three Fellows of Catherine Hall as trustees. Opposition from other beneficiaries and the misappropriation of funds by the one surviving trustee in the 1740s meant that the building of the hospital was much delayed, and it was not opened until 1776. Two new wings were added in 1823 and 37,181 patients had been treated by 1835.

Charity did much to advance education and to care for the sick during the eighteenth century. There was also much emphasis on the relief of poverty, but in this sphere it is striking that the poor rates were providing over two thirds of the funds as early as 1700. In the early nineteenth century politicians, social reformers and ratepayers became alarmed at the rising costs, and one of the aims of the Poor Law Amendment Act of 1834 was the reduction in overall expenditure. For almost three hundred years charity had been regarded as a means of social engineering, to placate the destitute who might otherwise pose a threat to society and to help them contribute to the well-being of the economy. Philanthropists of the nineteenth century had other aims. They reserved their help for those who would accept, or at least pay lip service to, certain moral standards. The emphasis changed from the state of mind of the giver to the moral character of the recipient.

SAINT BENEDICT SCHOOL
DUFFIELD ROAD
DERBY DE22 1JD

CHAPTER 3

CHARITY AS A MORAL RESPONSIBILITY

Nineteenth-century attitudes to charity

By 1800 the industrial and economic transformation of Britain was well under way, and a very rapid increase in population was in progress. Radical changes in work practices, overcrowding in the rapidly developing towns and the dislocation caused by the Napoleonic Wars gave rise to great distress, and there was an urgent need for effective relief. Eighteenth century rationalism was giving way to nineteenth century evangelism which permeated the voluntary enterprises of the time. Philanthropists became much more selective with regard to the recipients of their benefactions. Dr Andrew Reed, a Congregational minister, said this of one of the five charities he founded in the first half of the century:

> 'It is not intended to assist the worthless, the dissolute, or the mere pauper. The law of the land has provided sufficiently for them. It is meant to help those who would gladly have helped themselves, and others also, had not Divine Providence crossed their path by sudden and overwhelming calamity'.

The Victorian detestation of the idea of robbing people of their independence by 'pauperising' them unnecessarily was fully shared by Reed – and this possibility was probably no more palatable to the intended beneficiaries. Reed said that 'they cannot beg, for they have been accustomed to work; they refuse to be paupers, for they have wooed independence as their better life'.

Most busy industrial entrepreneurs found little time for philanthropy until the century was well advanced, but there were many - bankers, merchants, professional men and country gentlemen – who recognised the problems and were anxious to make a contribution towards their solution. Unfortunately the instruments for doing so were hopelessly inadequate.

The abuse of charitable status

Because of the multiplicity of obsolescent and overlapping trusts, existing charities were far from meeting contemporary needs. Trustees were often lazy or corrupt, and funds had been mismanaged or diverted from their original purposes. Some attempts were made to try to bring order to this chaos. For example, an 'Act for obliging Overseers of the Poor to make Returns upon Oath, to certain questions specified therein, relative to the State of the Poor' was passed in 1786.[23] The schedule to this act included questions asking how much money had been raised for relief of the poor in the previous three years, how many had benefited and how much had been spent on administration, expenses and 'entertainments'.

Justices of the peace were required to summon overseers of the poor to ensure that returns were made but, though non-compliance could incur heavy fines and even jail sentences, the Act was generally ignored. In 1812 an 'Act for the registering and securing of Charitable Donations' was passed.[25] The result of concern that many charitable donations 'appear to have been lost, and others from the Neglect of Payment and the Inattention of those Persons who ought to Superintend them', the Act required clerks of the peace to compile registers of charitable endowments for their districts. However, this Act, too, received but scant attention.

8. **John Scott, 1st earl of Eldon** (1751-1838) *c.*1828, studio of Sir Thomas Lawrence. Eldon was lord chancellor from 1801 to 1827 *(reproduced by kind permission of the National Portrait Gallery).*

The inadequacy of the courts and their processes

The commissions set up to enquire into abuses under the Statute of Charitable Uses (1601)[18] had long since become slow and inefficient, and new commissioners were rarely appointed. As noted earlier, litigants had for some time preferred to take their complaints to the attorney-general, the representative of the Crown which had the prerogative right to protect all charitable trusts, but by the late eighteenth century this alternative was proving even more tardy, costly and frustrating than acting through the

Elizabethan commissions. Many abuses were never brought to the attorney-general's attention; and even when they were, proceedings were seldom taken.

By now the Court of Chancery, which had started with such promise, had succumbed to the thrombosis which often afflicts long-standing institutions. Access was through such a multitude of sinecure offices and the procedures were so archaic and prolix that a charity might be ruined and a litigant die before a settlement was reached. Cases had accumulated as early as the sixteenth century, during the chancellorship of Cardinal Wolsey, and the ruthless clearing of the backlog by Sir Thomas More still aroused awed comment two generations later. In his *Utopia* a wordy lawyer is admonished 'Hold your peace' and, no doubt, the author would have been equally abrupt with legal long-windedness. Such dispatch was unusual in a chancellor and the court had relapsed into lethargy by the late eighteenth century, when a writer complained of the 'amicable gripe of the court of Chancery'. Soon after, the court became a byword for delay under Lord Eldon, chancellor from 1801 until 1827. A fine lawyer, responsible for many decisions that still govern charitable status, he believed that success could only be achieved by living like a hermit and working like a horse. He had eloped with a banker's daughter when he was twenty-one and seemed wary of haste ever afterwards. Below is an example of his convoluted and conservative style – on this occasion when refusing to alter the purpose of the charitable trust for Leeds Grammar School so that French, German and other subjects useful in commerce could be taught:[65]

'I do not apprehend, it is competent to this court, as long as it can find any means of applying the charitable fund to the charity as created by the founder, upon any general notion, that any other application would be more beneficial to the inhabitants of the place, to change the nature of the charity'

Lord Eldon did point out that the change proposed would benefit the thriving merchants of Leeds rather than poor students, but, by ruling that the original purpose was immutable, he hampered the modernisation of educational charities for many years. The court he had presided over was thus described by Dickens in the middle of the century: 'never can there come fog too thick, never can there come mud and mire too deep, to assort with the groping and floundering condition which this High Court of Chancery, most pestilent of hoary sinners, holds, this day, in the sight of heaven and earth'

The Brougham Commission

It was not unknown for Dickens to exaggerate in order to force home his points, but he was by no means the first to complain. Sir Samuel Romilly had made great efforts to circumvent the law's delays and his Act 'to provide a summary Remedy in Cases of Abuses of Trusts created for Charitable Purposes' was passed in 1812.[24] It was intended to expedite and reduce the cost of trust proceedings and so make it less likely that charities would be ruined by vindictive petitioners. It did not have the desired effect, because even minor cases involved Chancery and, as Romilly said in Parliament in 1818, it was 'impossible, through the Court of Chancery, to obtain redress for the abuses of charitable institutions'.[66] Another M.P. complained that 'Many families were ruined with the very best cause before a decision could be given'.

Henry Brougham made a strong denunciation: 'he allowed those courts the possession of learning without stint. He allowed them great copiousness, great powers of drawing out written argument. The faculty of caring nothing for the time and patience of suitors and the hundreds of thousands of their clients money they enjoyed in a perfection which the wildest sallies of the imagination could not go beyond'

9.   The Foundling Restored to its Mother, by Emma Brownlow. John Brownlow, in the centre of the picture, was himself a foundling; he became secretary to the Foundling Hospital, and the artist was his daughter *(reproduced by kind permission of the Thomas Coram Foundation for Children)*.

With public opinion behind him, Brougham campaigned successfully for a parliamentary committee to investigate charitable trusts, and this was authorised by the Charitable Foundations Act.[27] This Act did not afford all the powers which Brougham wanted, as the House of Lords managed to limit the investigation to educational charities only – admittedly, an area where malpractice was widespread. Brougham's belief that the very setting up of the commission would be sufficient to spur trustees into mending their ways was misplaced. The Royal Commission to Inquire concerning Charities for the Education of the Poor,[26] which reported between 1819 and 1837, found that thousands of endowments were still being misdirected.

The Commission unearthed information about a very large number of day schools. Of these some 14,300 were not endowed; they had about 310,000 fee paying and 168,000 charity-supported pupils. Over 4,100 schools, with about 165,000 pupils, were endowed. There were also a small number of endowed elementary schools which had been founded by Nonconformists, Quakers, Jews and Huguenots. In the first half of the nineteenth century the very idea of providing education for the poor, even if privately funded, was by no means generally accepted. When Samuel Whitbread's Education Bill of 1807 was being debated, one M.P. complained that 'it would in effect be prejudicial to their morals and happiness; it would teach them to despise their lot in life'. One solution would have been to levy a compulsory rate for education but it was suspected that, while all would pay, only schools supported by the Established Church would benefit. Such suspicions were not unfounded, as those with influence in this field were usually fervent champions of the Anglican Church. Despite the Toleration Act of 1689[21] and the Roman Catholic Relief Act of 1829,[27] which removed disabilities from dissenters and papists respectively, Lord Eldon and his successors, when adjudicating on charitable gifts which had been bequeathed in loosely worded wills, strained the law in favour of the Church of England.

The role of charity in nineteenth century education

In 1814 the Government took a first timid step towards state funding of education when the Kildare Place Society was authorised to disburse a small parliamentary grant of £6,890. In 1833 £20,000 was handed directly to two societies involved in educating the poor – the National Society for Promoting the Education of the Poor in the Principles of the Established Church (founded in 1811), and the British and Foreign Schools Society, set up by Nonconformists in 1814.

Late in the eighteenth century, Robert Raikes, appalled at the behaviour of the young tearaways in Gloucester on their one day free from grinding labour, had set up Sunday Schools where children might learn to read and repeat the catechism. Schools run by both the National and the British and Foreign Societies were a little more ambitious. They used the monitorial system (developed independently by Dr Andrew Bell, an Anglican, and Joseph Lancaster, a Quaker) whereby selected older children ('monitors') passed on instruction, given them by the master, to the younger children. It was extremely cheap to operate, as few masters were needed and apparatus was simple – for example, sand tables (used for arithmetic calculations) which were smoothed over at the end of each lesson. A child could be taught for as little as seven shillings a year, but instruction was strictly regimented with few educational tools. In 1847-8 government inspectors reported that there was too much emphasis on religious instruction and too few good books on secular subjects; also, that in many schools there were no blackboards, maps or globes and insufficient aids to arithmetic, drawing and singing.

In 1824 the British and Foreign Schools Society had been enterprising enough to take over the New Lanark School (founded by Robert Owen in 1816) with its pioneering emphasis on illustration, story telling and natural history based on life in the neighbourhood. By 1861 it had become relatively less active, and administered fewer than 10 per cent of inspected schools, whereas the National Society ran over 76 per cent, the remaining 14% being run by Wesleyans, Congregationalists, Roman Catholics and others. These schools were mainly funded by voluntary contributions and, though limited by lack of funds, they tried to provide a rudimentary education. Others, however, were no more than working schools, training children for such tasks as operating spinning machinery in Northern England or producing straw plait for the Luton hat trade, often selling the products of their work.

The grammar schools had other difficulties. Though they might be well endowed, the misuse of trust funds for education was particularly blatant – as, for instance, when masters had no pupils but still drew a salary. Often they were tied by the terms of the trust deed to an outdated curriculum, which proved difficult to amend due to the conservatism of decrees in Chancery. Sir Eardley Wilmot's Act of 1840[30] aimed to give the governing bodies of grammar schools a freer hand in interpreting trust provisions. It also authorised courts of inquiry to revise systems of administration and curricula, but only 'if it shall be found necessary from the Insufficiency of the Revenues'. Such limited powers proved ineffective, abuses continued, and it was eventually decided to take further measures. The Endowed Schools Act of 1869[35] empowered three independent commissioners to reorganise trusts over fifty years old, without applying to the trustees or even taking the wishes of the original donor into account. The commissioners could also apply to education, money which was originally intended for such outmoded objects as doles, marriage portions and 'redemption of prisoners and captives'. This was a great departure from past practice, and it indicates how seriously the abuses were regarded. Ninety years later the Nathan Committee thought this 'still constitutes the greatest breach in the cy-pres doctrine'.[59]

The establishment of the Charity Commission

At first the Brougham Commission could only investigate educational charities but, as time passed, it obtained additional powers to examine other types of charities as well. Though the costs of the enquiry were high by contemporary standards (reaching £208,000 by 1835), the final report made recommendations which were considered important enough to be implemented. The commission wished to see investigations into the administration of all charitable trusts, with the powers of trustees supplemented if they were inadequate for efficient management. Charities were to be compelled to produce audited accounts from time to time, and in future trust funds should be properly invested and kept in safe custody. Legal proceedings were to be brought under proper control, and made easier and cheaper to undertake. Finally, the report recommended that the Elizabethan county commissions should be replaced by a central Board of Commissioners to supervise charitable trusts throughout the country.

Despite their moderation these proposals indicate the appalling confusion that existed, but this was a time when any government intervention was regarded with suspicion: many agreed with Thomas Paine that 'government, even in its best state, is but a necessary evil', and the philanthropist Andrew Reed wrote 'so that it is done, the more the people do, and the less it [the Government] does, the better'. Despite this attitude, the immense labours of the Brougham Commission came to fruition with the Charitable Trusts Act of 1853.[31] This authorised the appointment of three commissioners who 'so holding Office during good Behaviour shall be paid as herein-after mentioned, and Two at least of the said paid Commissioners for the Time being shall be Barristers-at-Law of not less than Twelve Years standing [with power] to examine or inquire into all or any Charities in England and Wales'.

The fourth, unpaid, commissioner was Sir George Grey, about to become Colonial Secretary, who would represent the commission in Parliament. The commissioners appointed two inspectors who could examine trustees under oath and require the production of documents. The powers of the commissioners extended to endowed charities only and not to those 'wholly maintained by voluntary contributions'. Great hopes must have been pinned on the new organisation, as the commissioners and inspectors were all experienced and able men, but it had to operate under formidable difficulties.

By 1854 there had been many applications for the appointment or removal of trustees and for the establishment of new trusts. These had involved a lot of work, as small charities in particular had submitted proposals without the benefit of professional advice. Yet the commission had no power to establish schemes itself and was obliged to work through the attorney-general using the existing legal machinery. Additional legislation was needed, but this proved very hard to obtain. In both Houses of Parliament there were groups who did not wish for any change and they could mount strong opposition from well entrenched positions.

For example, many obsolete and inefficient but profitable charities were in church hands, and the bench of Bishops had no wish to see them reformed. One scandalous example was the richly-endowed Hospital of St Cross at Winchester, founded in 1136 by that belligerent bishop, Henry of Blois, a grandson of the Conqueror. It was alleged that the original deeds and registers had been burned and, in 1686, a new document for the administration of the hospital had been drawn up by the master. Complaints about abuses came before the Queen's Bench in 1851, when a judge called this document 'bare-faced and shameless' and 'a wilful breach of trust'. Perhaps Hiram's Hospital at Barchester, and its doughty defender Archdeacon Grantley, whose 'very gait is a speaking sermon', were typical of Trollope's time? Eventually, the commissioners were obliged to fall back on the time-consuming and less radical solutions offered by the Court of Chancery, using the *cy-pres* doctrine.

Extending the powers of the Charity Commission

However, at least one provision of the Act was to operate with great success. It set up an Official Trustee of Charitable Funds and authorised charities to hand funds to him for safe-keeping and investment. Such transfers cost nothing but they had to be approved by the courts and, in their second annual report, the commissioners pleaded for this restriction to be removed. This was done in 1855 when the Charitable Trusts (Amendment) Act was passed.[33] By 1858 £406,082 had been transferred and, ten years later, this had risen to £3,443,030. This Act also ensured that private persons wishing to take out suits against charities had to initiate proceedings through the Charity Commission. This gave the commission an opportunity to intervene before application was made to the attorney-general and so, it was hoped, reduced the amount of needless litigation.

The Commissioners obtained further additional powers by the Charitable Trusts Act of 1860.[34] Even for a small charity, recourse to Chancery cost £50 on average and the Act was intended to provide an inexpensive substitute by empowering the commission 'to make orders such as now be made by any Judge of the Court of Chancery'. This enabled the commission to appoint and remove trustees and to alter trusts, although if the charity's annual income was over £50 the consent of the majority of the trustees had to be obtained. There was also a right of appeal to the courts against the decisions of the commission. Despite these constraints the commission exercised supervision over 80 per cent of charities by the 1880s, but many of these were small. As at that time 10 per cent of endowments accounted for about 85 per cent of charitable funds, the commission had little influence over most of the income.

For very many years trustees had sometimes been found personally liable for breaches of trust, as in a case in 1720 when there was a misapplication of increased revenues[67] and in 1835 when a dissenting chapel was converted for use by a sect contrary to the founder's wishes.[68] The problem became more serious in 1854 when, to speed the dispatch of business in the Court of Chancery when there were delays due to death or change of ownership, an Act[32] was passed which enabled the common law courts to intervene and to award costs out of the funds involved in the suit. In 1872 the Charitable Trustees Incorporation Act[36] authorised the Charity Commissioners to register trustees of any charity as a corporate body which then controlled the assets, but this did not absolve the trustees from accountability for their own actions. It was not until the Trustee Act[41] was passed in 1925 that trustees were given some protection from personal liability for claims made on a charity.

Reorganising and amalgamating charities

The financial institutions of the City of London had a reputation for managing charitable funds efficiently, and this persuaded many donors, including the eccentrics, to entrust endowments to liveried companies. By 1880 these companies controlled a trust income of about £200,000, of which about £75,000 went to almshouses and pensions, about £75,000 to education, and about £50,000 to other purposes, some of them obsolete. The City of London and Parochial Charities Act of 1883[37] empowered the Charity Commissioners (reinforced by an additional commissioner) to review all City charities and to reapportion funds from 'moribund' parishes with small populations but large endowments to parishes with large populations but small endowments. Once the commissioners had set guidelines and done the preliminary legal work, the large parishes were left to manage their own affairs.

The moribund parishes were, however, relieved of many of their responsibilities; day-to-day management passed to the Trustees of the London Parochial Charities, on which the Crown and the City Corporations were well represented. The income was to be used to provide education, libraries, museums, open spaces, provident institutions, convalescent hospitals and other facilities for 'poorer inhabitants of the metropolis'. Endowments less than fifty years old were not affected, and the powers conferred on the Charity Commissioners by the 1883 Act lapsed in 1889. Even so, in 1914 the Charity Commissioners were authorised to extend the 'beneficial area' of City charities outwards where movements of population justified this.

The ancient Statute of Charitable Uses of 1601[18] was repealed by the Mortmain and Charitable Uses Act in 1888.[31] This Act and later legislation in 1891[39] were intended to mitigate the harsh terms of the Mortmain Act 1736,[22] by authorising limited companies and some other corporations to hold land without licence in mortmain. Nevertheless, strict conditions remained: any land conveyed to a charity without royal licence or statutory authority became forfeit to the Crown; lands had to be willed at least twelve months, and stock in public funds at least six months, before death; and if the land was held as an investment, it had to be sold within one year after the testator's death. If, on the other hand, it was for use by the charity the court or the Charity Commissioners might sanction its retention. Land for public parks (twenty acres or less), elementary schoolhouses (one acre or less) and public museums (two acres or less) was exempt from the provisions of the Act. The 1888 and 1891 Acts were both revoked by the Charities Act of 1960.

The status of non-endowed charities

By the mid-nineteenth century, therefore, charities endowed as trusts were supervised by the Charity Commissioners and under the jurisdiction of the Court of Chancery. Other voluntary undertakings were, however, outside the scope of charitable legislation, and as a result there was much duplication of purpose. Some charities were dubious and others were undoubtedly fraudulent. This situation offended the businesslike and righteous Victorians and several private societies were formed to exercise charitable functions in a proper and seemly fashion. In Liverpool, for example, where systems of casual labour were very widespread, employers seldom had close ties with their workers

10. The Court of Chancery, by Benjamin Ferrers. This view shows the court in session during the reign of George I. At that time the courts of chancery and king's bench were still held in Westminster Hall and the figures in the foreground are probably making their way to the other court. On the bench there are probably Lord Chancellor Macclesfield (beneath the royal arms), flanked by Sir Philip Yorke (the solicitor-general) and Sir Thomas Pengelly (king's prime sergeant) *(reproduced by kind permission of the National Portrait Gallery)*.

and, though munificent gifts were made – such as the Brown Library and the Walker Gallery – help for the needy came not from paternalistic industrialists but from organised voluntary effort.

Several of these voluntary societies had overlapping functions, and they were combined and rationalised when the Central Relief Society was founded in 1863. It continued to bring relief direct to those in need. The Society for Organising Charitable Relief and Repressing Mendicity, started somewhat later, maintai   little contact with beneficiaries, though it had more ambitious administrative   s. The original prospectus was drafted by John Ruskin and, although its first presic   it was the bishop of London, it became a national organisation. Known as the Charity Organisation Society, or C.O.S. for short, it set out to reorganise the whole charitable movement, eventually declaring its policies in its annual report for 1877.[69]

It wished to define the boundary between public relief and private charity and 'to bring into harmonious co-operation with each other and with the Poor-Law authorities the various charitable agencies'. The society thought that voluntary charities should deny assistance to those receiving support under the Poor Law, because this would discourage pauperism. It offered 'to investigate thoroughly the cases of all applicants for charitable relief [and] to place gratuitously at the disposal of the charitable agencies and private persons the investigating machinery of the Committee of the Society'. It then intended 'to obtain from the proper charities, or from charitable individuals, suitable and adequate relief for deserving cases'. As a main principle it wished 'to promote...the general welfare of the poor by means of social and sanitary reforms, and by the inculcation of habits of providence and self-dependence [and] to repress mendicity...by the prosecution of impostors'. Finally, a general wish to promote charitable giving meant that it would 'afford to the public at large information regarding the objects and mode of working of existing charities'.

An early success was scored with its cautionary lists of bogus charities which, despite fervent protests, the courts refused to declare as libellous. Yet, having no close contact with those in need, the C.O.S. may have become doctrinaire, even complacent, and its aloof stance was exposed when the name of Dr Barnado, esteemed for his deep understanding and love of children, appeared on one of these lists. Barnado, with his extraordinary flair for publicity, had achieved much for his charities but his accounting methods were open to question and, despite the offence caused, a committee was appointed to 'advise' him. From then on the massive funds he raised were distributed in a less arbitrary and more business-like way.

Although the C.O.S. had no compunction about leaving the 'undeserving' to the mercies of the Poor Law, it had other policies which were less questionable. During the 1890s, for example, it put pressure on the Government to form a Central Hospital Board. This was unsuccessful but its arguments may have found favour elsewhere, for in 1897 the Prince of Wales founded what was to become King Edward's Hospital Fund, which worked towards rationalisation and greater efficiency of hospital services. By 1900 the C.O.S. had spread its influence nationally, operating through about forty district committees. Nevertheless it must have been disappointed that so little progress was made towards coordinating the work of charities, most of which seemed determined to maintain their independence even when this led to inefficiency. In 1946 the society was reconstituted as the Family Welfare Association, and as such is still in operation.

Refining the definition of charitable purposes

Meanwhile many charitable initiatives had been taken elsewhere in England and Wales. for example, the Hospital Sunday Fund, which used money from church collections to support hospitals, had been organised in Birmingham; the District Nursing movement, which eventually employed about 7,300 nurses in 1000 associations throughout the country, was started by William Rathbone of Liverpool in the early 1860s: a training school and home for nurses was established in cooperation with Liverpool Infirmary in 1862. His scheme had enthusiastic support from Florence Nightingale, who demanded that a district nurse must be 'a sanitary missionary' and not a mere clothes-giver or soup-giver, and who sent a wreath to Rathbone's funeral inscribed 'One of God's best and greatest sons'.

Although there was clearly a great deal of activity among voluntary organisations, decisions about the status of charitable trusts were still being arrived at by finding analogies from the list contained in the preamble to the Statute of Charitable Uses of 1601.[18] In 1805 Samuel Romilly, appearing for the next-of-kin who were contesting a bequest to charity,[70] had tried to define a degree of order in this procedure: 'there are four objects, within one of which all Charity to be administered in this Court, must fall: 1st, Relief of the indigent; in various ways: Money: Provisions: Education: Medical assistance etc: 2dly, the Advancement of Learning: 3rdly, the Advancement of Religion: and 4thly, which is the most difficult, the advancement of objects of general public utility'.

In 1891[71] Lord Macnaghten simplified these four categories of charitable uses by listing them as the relief of poverty; the advancement of religion; the advancement of education; and other uses of benefit to the public. Modern legislation is still based on this grouping and the Elizabethan statute.

Some applications of the *cy-pres* doctrine

The ancient *cy-pres* doctrine was still being applied. Thomas Betton, in his will of 15 February 1723, left 'one full half part of the said interest and profit of my whole estate, yearly and every year for ever into the redemption of British Slaves in Turkey or Barbary'. The income of about £1000 a year accumulated and by 1844 the trustees, the Ironmongers' Company, had £100,000 of 3% stock but could find no slaves to ransom. As funds had also been left for Church of England schools, the courts decided that the funds in question should be transferred for that purpose.[72] In another case, heard in 1937, the founder's intentions could not be implemented in the first place, as money was left to a non-existent 'Newcastle-upon-Tyne Nursing Home'.[73] As the bequest was sandwiched between other charitable bequests it was decided that the money could be applied to charities. In 1947 the trustees of the Dominican Students' Hall Trust were permitted to delete 'of European origin' from the memorandum of the association to avoid offence.[74] On the other hand, in 1950 part of a residuary estate was left for purchasing land and erecting rest houses.[75] The bequest proved insufficient for this purpose and, as no general charitable intent was evident, the gift lapsed.

War charities

A special category of charities was that created by the War Charities Acts, that of 1916 being superseded by that of 1940.[42] In the later Act the principal object of a 'War Charity' was defined as the relief of distress and suffering caused by the 1914-18 war, the current war, or any war which the sovereign by Order in Council declared to be applicable. The Act defined which local authorities were qualified to register war charities, and fund raising appeals from non-registered charities were prohibited. War charities were subject to controls similar to those imposed on other charities but, foreshadowing the Charities Act 1992, it was an offence to raise money without the approval in writing of the war charity concerned. Apart from the 1940 Act the war had little effect on the management of charitable institutions. The real challenge was to come after 1945, when the very existence of voluntary charities was called into question.

CHAPTER 4

CHARITY IN THE WELFARE STATE

The role of charity and the Nathan Committee

Today, when social welfare is mainly funded by the state, it is easy to forget the major role played by voluntary organisations in the past. The Nathan Committee,[59] investigating charitable trusts during 1950-52, was impressed: 'One of the magnificent failures of our history is the endeavour made by these charities, more particularly in the late eighteenth and in the nineteenth century, to provide by private effort universal services of schools, hospitals, dispensaries, almshouses, orphanages, pensions for the aged and relief for other categories of the "deserving poor" '.

State intervention had been gradual. There had been statutory relief for the poor since Tudor times but very little for education, for example, until the latter half of the nineteenth century. State education became firmly established early in this century, and the National Insurance Act was passed in 1911, but the most sweeping changes occurred after 1945. Wide-ranging social legislation was introduced by the Labour Government and, when the Nathan Committee was set up, some believed that with 'statutory services, new and old, which now provided for the welfare of the individual from the cradle to the grave...the basic question confronting the Committee was what remained for charities to do'. The chairman, Lord Nathan, an eminent lawyer and parliamentarian, took a different view. He thought the committee's assignment was 'to recommend ways in which the goodwill of the past may be more free to serve the changing needs of the present'.

The committee soon recognised that the mutual exclusiveness of voluntary and statutory services was a thing of the past, with no clear distinction between them because 'historically state action is voluntary action crystallised and made universal'. It was concluded that 'so far from voluntary action being dried up by the extension of the social services greater and greater demands are being made on it. We believe, indeed, that the democratic state, as we know it, could hardly function effectively...without such channels for, and demands upon, voluntary services'.

It was recommended that the state system should be supplemented by voluntary efforts which could be expected to stimulate, restrain and criticise statutory bodies. 'I think it is the business of trusts to live dangerously', said the secretary of the Carnegie United Kingdom Trust when giving evidence to the committee, and the committee agreed with him. It was seen that the voluntary sector – which, unlike government departments, had freedom to experiment – could pioneer new initiatives which the state might take over if they proved beneficial.

The committee argued that, if voluntary charity was to be encouraged, charitable trusts must be allowed to retain their ancient privileges: the rights to exist in perpetuity, to have vague testamentary dispositions made precisely worded, and to define fresh objects if those originally laid down were or became incapable of execution. They even recommended relaxation of the *cy-pres* doctrine, to place all charitable trusts on the same footing as those for education – endowed schools had, under various Acts, been given greater freedom to revise their trust deeds, with little regard for the founder's wishes, if these had become outdated.

Implementing the recommendations of the Nathan Committee

The Nathan Committee was also concerned about the difficulties experienced by organisations with a mixture of charitable and non-charitable purposes. For example, the Oxford Group[76] had been found liable to income tax in 1949 as, although the advancement of the Christian religion in accordance with the principles of the Movement was held to be charitable, the support of the Movement and its associates in every way was not. The committee suggested that such trusts should be able to transfer non-charitable funds to a valid trust, provided that they had been set up at least six years previously. On the other hand, it saw no reason why those drawing up trust deeds after 1949 should be protected from their own ignorance and, indeed, considered that new trusts should be subject to more stringent tests than in the past. This was especially important if there were other beneficiaries.

These recommendations resulted in the Charitable Trusts (Validation) Act of 1954,[45] which defined an imperfect trust provision as one where 'property could be used exclusively for charitable purposes, but could nevertheless be used for purposes which are not charitable'. The Act aimed to help existing trusts with constitutions of doubtful legality but it was also intended to bear down hard on future victims of bad draftsmanship. The Act has been held to validate trusts for the welfare of employees and of trade union members which might otherwise be considered as not benefiting a sufficient section of the public.[77] It was, however, limited in scope, and several judges found its terms difficult to construe. For example, after the Gillingham bus disaster in 1959 the mayors of surrounding towns 'decided to promote a Royal Marine Cadet Corps Memorial Fund to be devoted, among other things, to defraying the funeral expenses, caring for the boys who may be disabled, and to such worthy cause or causes...as the Mayors may determine'. The third purpose was considered to render the trust void for uncertainty, and the 1954 Act did not save it, although one judge disagreed.[78]

The 1960 Charities Act[47] incorporated many of the Nathan Committee's recommendations. It greatly simplified charitable legislation by repealing the Mortmain Acts and all the Charitable Trusts Acts passed between 1853 and 1939. The Charity Commission was reconstituted and strengthened; although the number of commissioners was to remain at three, one or two additional commissioners could be appointed if the Treasury agreed. They were to be appointed by the home secretary, who was to represent the commission in Parliament. For the first time the functions of the commissioners were defined: to promote the effective use of charitable resources by encouraging better administration; by investigating and checking abuses; and by advising trustees. There were provisions for such advice to be challenged and, for this reason, it was later ruled that no proceedings could be taken against the Charity Commissioners for giving unsatisfactory advice.

New roles for the Charity Commission

A Central Register of Charities was to be established although very small charities were exempt from this requirement. Some others, specifically listed in the second schedule, were also exempted. Those already controlled by other means were known as 'excepted charities'. These included charities founded under the Companies Acts, by special Acts of Parliament, by royal charter or by persons acting under royal charter or royal licence. Local authorities were to be allowed to form local registers and review charities in their area, with a view to future collaboration between different charities and between charities and local authorities.

The circumstances in which *cy-pres* schemes could be effected by the court or the Charity Commissioners were set out in some detail. Charitable property could be applied *cy-pres* where the original purpose had been fulfilled, could not be carried out or used only part of the property; where it could be more effectively used when combined with other trust funds; where an area of benefit or a class of persons to benefit had ceased to exist or to be considered suitable for help; or where the purpose was now provided by other means or was considered useless or harmful.

The commissioners were given jurisdiction, concurrent with that of the High Court, for drawing up constitutions, appointing or removing trustees or officers, and transferring property of charities. These powers could only be exercised if an application was made by the charity concerned; or if an order was made by the court; or if the charity had an annual income of not more than £50; or if the trustees unreasonably refused or neglected to draw up a scheme – but this could not be done until forty years after the charity had been founded, five years more than the Nathan Committee had recommended. It was later ruled that plaintiffs in charity proceedings must have an interest materially greater than, or different from, an ordinary member of the public.[79, 80]

It is doubtful whether charities have any real claim to being considered under equity but, after the Judicature Acts of 1873-5 combined both common law and equity into one set of courts with each judge having both jurisdictions, charities were still dealt with in the Chancery Division. The Supreme Court Act of 1981[54] specifically assigned cases concerned with charitable trusts to that division.

Charity lands and finances in the late twentieth century

The repeal of the 1891 Mortmain and Charitable Uses Act[39] in 1960 meant that charities were not obliged to sell donated land within one year. This considerably reduced the work of the commission which no longer had to check that sales had actually been made. Professor Keeton described the 1960 act as 'possibly the most important enactment upon the law of charities' since 1601, and many of its provisions have been included in the most recent legislation. Yet some trustees expected too much of it, wrongly imagining that it would allow radical changes to trust deeds so that the urgent needs of today could be satisfied. In 1961 the Commissioners reported that 'We have frequently to explain that the doctrine of cy-pres...requires the new purpose to be as near as possible to those prescribed by the donor'.

At a time of rapidly rising inflation, particular attention had to be given to charity investments. In mediaeval times the only form of property capable of producing income was land and, up to the eighteenth century, the usual endowment of a charity was either land or rents from land. The Mortmain Act 1736 was introduced because it was feared that too much land would fall into the 'dead hand' of charity but, as a counterbalance, the courts authorised the investment of trust money in 'the public funds'. During the nineteenth century it also became possible to invest in a 'trustee list' of fixed interest stocks backed by the government or other first class credit agencies. Such investments retained their value, more or less, until they became seriously eroded by inflation after 1940. The Trustee Investment Act of 1961[48] permitted trustees, unless specifically prohibited by the trust deed, to invest in equities as well as government and fixed interest stocks. In fact, trustees were encouraged to do so as part of their duty to maintain the value of charity property. However only half of the funds available could be invested in the 'riskier' funds.

This relaxation posed problems. There was a danger that large quantities of undated gilt-edged investments would be thrown on to an already saturated market by charities anxious to switch into equities. Under the 1960 Charities Act the commissioners were authorised to set up 'common investment funds' for those charities, particularly small ones, which might prefer to pool their investments with those of other similar charities.

The Charity Commissioners realised the need for such an expertly-managed fund, especially when they found, after making enquiries in 1962, that about £15 million was available for investment as opposed to the £5 million originally envisaged. The Charities' Official Investment Fund was set up by the Official Custodian of Charities, who fulfilled functions similar to those formerly undertaken by the Official Trustees. Eventually this fund held investments worth £1.25 billion on behalf of forty thousand charities.

With the exception of trusts for strictly limited purposes, which can come to an end,[81] charities have the privilege of perpetual existence. However, until 1964 they were bound by a rule against perpetuities which governed the vesting of interests and not their duration. A 'perpetuity period' was defined as that covering 'lives in being plus 21 years'. Before the Perpetuities and Accumulation Act of 1964[50] came into force any trust was void if it did not have to take effect within the perpetuity period – for example, if there was an indefinite failure of issue within a particular family. The law held that gifts from a charity to a non-charity must occur during the perpetuity period.

The 1964 Act made it possible to specify and define a perpetuity period up to a maximum of eighty years, and thus greatly to reduce the ambiguities inherent in the previous vague procedure. Nevertheless, a gift which is subject to the occurrence of a certain event may still be declared void. An example of this type of situation is provided by the case of the Honourable Mary Howard's deed of 13 April 1864, leaving land and buildings for use as an orphan girls' home at Kendal. The home had to close in 1954 and, as the property had been left 'for no other trust or purpose whatsoever' it could not be applied to some other purpose *cy-pres* – that is, no other interpretation or re-wording of the original gift was possible, and as a result the property had to revert to the estate.[82]

In their turn, charities may refuse to accept gifts because they object to conditions made by donors. In such a case the court may modify the objectionable condition, or the gift may go to another charity willing to comply with it. Otherwise the gift lapses if there is no apparent general charitable intent. In 1981 a bequest to set up music scholarships was rejected by two colleges of music, as it was restricted to orphans who stood very good chances of obtaining grants elsewhere. There was a *cy-pres* modification so that the scholarships went to those who could not get them otherwise, and in this form they were acceptable to the charities in question.[83]

The problem of small charities

For many years there had been concern about charities with small endowments which produced, in real terms, ever-decreasing incomes. Although there had been opportunities to amalgamate some small charities – for example the twenty-six charities which were combined to form the Winchester Rural Welfare Trust – the provisions of the Charities Act 1960 had generally been too rigidly applied. During the 1970s the Charity Commissioners had to point out that, in order for amalgamation to take place, the purposes of such charities did not have to be identical, only similar. The Charities Act of 1985[55] was supposed to build on these provisions so that trustees of local and small charities could make better use of their funds. However, the Act proved ineffective as its procedures were too complex and restrictive.

It was replaced by two provisions of the Charities Act of 1992[57] which enabled trustees of a small charity to transfer assets to one or more other charities with similar aims and to amend the objects and administrative powers of that charity; and also to spend its permanent endowments and so terminate the charitable trust. Under the 1985 Act all the trustees had to agree to such proceedings and such schemes could not be introduced until at least fifty years after the foundation of the charity. Under the 1992 Act only a two-thirds majority was required and there was no moratorium period. But trustees did have to be satisfied that the purposes of the charity were no longer an effective application of its resources.

During the nineteenth century the fear that charities might accumulate vast areas of land seems to have receded. Indeed, owners were positively encouraged to donate land for charitable purposes by such legislation as the School Sites Act 1841, the Literary and Scientific Institutions Act 1854, and the Places of Worship Act 1873. Because owners might be worried about the fate of such lands if they ceased to be used for the intended charitable purposes, it was ruled that in such circumstances the property would revert to the original owners or their heirs. However, when this happened trustees had no power to sell or repair such properties, and the Reverter of Sites Act 1987[56] enabled trusts to be set up to manage, repair or sell the land on behalf of the reverter. Problems might still arise if the land had been transferred to the Official Custodian, and these were dealt with by the Charities Act 1992[57] which empowered the Charity Commissioners to transfer the land back to the trustees.

11. The preamble to the original manuscript copy of the Statute of Charitable Uses, 1601, with the royal assent ('La Royne Le Veult') *(the Act is in the custody of the House of Lords Record Office and is reproduced by kind permission of the Clerk of the Records).*

Supervision and control - an impossible task?

'The altruistic world of charity has attracted some rather grubby elements', said one noble lord during a debate in 1991. He should not have been surprised, as charitable funds had continually been misapplied since the days of the chantries, but certainly there was greater reason for concern as by the early 1990s vast sums of money were involved. Since 1960 there had been considerable growth in charitable activity and by 1992 there were over 170,000 registered charities with a total turnover of about £17 billion – more than the whole output of Britain's largest industry, agriculture. Moreover, the Charity Commission no longer had the resources to maintain effective control of such a large and expanding sector of the economy. As early as 1975 it had to report that inclusion on its central register offered no guarantee that it approved of the objects of a charity or that the institution was properly run by trustees and officers of good character - adequate checking and supervision was simply impossible.

It was widely feared that the existing legislation was inadequate to cope with any abuses which might arise, and in 1985 the National Council for Voluntary Organisations reviewed methods currently available for protection against dubious practices. In 1987 an 'Efficiency Scrutiny of the Supervision of Charities' [84] was carried out by a group chaired by Sir Philip Woodfield. The recommendations of this body were largely implemented in the Charities Act 1992,[57] which dealt not with the legal status of charities but with the operations carried out by them or on their behalf.

The Act of 1992

Before effective control could be imposed it was necessary to remedy the defects in the Central Register. Exempt charities, which were outside the Commission's control, had hitherto been able to register on a voluntary basis. The Act put a stop to this. 'Small' charities did not have to register, but the definition of magnitude had been based on investment income. This might have been appropriate in the past, when most charities had relied on endowments, but many of those founded more recently had no endowment income but raised considerable annual incomes from subscriptions – and these had been excused from registering. To end this anomaly the new criterion for registration was based on income from all sources. After transfer to computer the reorganised and more accessible register was a very useful tool when implementing the additional powers conferred by the 1992 Act.

For example the Commission could now refuse to register a charity with a name similar to that of another charity, and the improved Register allowed it to make the necessary checks more readily. Names which might mislead the public about the objects of a charity were banned, and charities with a gross income of £5,000 or more were obliged to give their registration number on certain documents, which made it harder to distribute fraudulent prospectuses. Although it had never done so before, after 1992 the Charity Commission was to charge for registration and other services.

Charities now had to submit annual accounts and reports to the Commission automatically without being asked. All accounts had to be audited or, for smaller charities, at least examined by a suitably qualified independent person. There were provisions for dealing with the assets of 'dormant' charities which had ceased to function. The investigative powers of the Charity Commissioners were increased: they could already demand information when conducting an investigation, but now they could call for it in connection with any of their functions, and not just from charities – Government departments and statutory bodies were also obliged to supply information.

It became an offence to give the Charity Commission false information. Where malpractice was suspected the commissioners were authorised to take immediate action to protect charity property – even before misconduct or maladministration had been established. For the first time the commissioners were empowered to initiate civil proceedings, though they were recommended to obtain the prior consent of the attorney-general.

The new roles of the Charity Commission and trustees

The Charity Commission increased its investigation and monitoring staff and during 1992 over seven hundred enquiries were completed, about half dealing with maladministration and about a quarter with malpractice. Fifty-one cases were referred to the police. Such work was considered of prime importance and, so that the Charity Commissioners could concentrate on it, many responsibilities were handed back to the trustees of charities. Once again they could deal with disposals of charity land and the consent of the commissioners was only required if a disposal was to someone closely associated with the charity. Trustees became more responsible for managing charitable investments and the free investment service provided by the Official Custodian was withdrawn. He was also required to divest himself of investments held on behalf of charities, although this did not include land or any assets transferred to him for the protection of a charity. About £1.25 billion was then held on behalf of about forty thousand charities, and it was recognised that the divesting of assets would take five years to complete. At the same time trustees were allowed a wider choice of investments and the home secretary was empowered to authorise additional types of equities for investment and to increase the proportion of funds that could be invested in them.

It was recognised that the additional responsibilities thus imposed on trustees might encourage some charities to seek incorporation, and the Charitable Trustees Incorporation Act 1872[36] was amended to make it easier to do so. To increase supervisory control over such charitable companies the Charity Commission was empowered to intervene in their affairs and its approval had to be sought before passing resolutions concerning service agreements or the use of company property.

It was hoped that, by increasing their responsibilities, trustees would be encouraged to take a more active interest in the charities they managed. That such encouragement was often necessary is instanced by the activities of an employee of the National Hospital for Neurology and Neurosurgery Development Foundation, who misappropriated around £2.7 million by forging signatures for building society accounts and diverting funds into another account outside the control of the charity. Supervision had been lax and the irregularities had not been identified by the auditors, who agreed to make a substantial contribution to the charity. Happily the trustees managed to recover most of the money.

The provisions described so far were contained in Part I of the Charities Act 1992. Other parts of the Act provided for more effective supervision of fundraising activities, not by the Charity Commission but by the charities themselves.

Fundraising and professional employees

Many charities were employing professionals fund raisers who, in some cases, were retaining excessive sums for their own remuneration. An investigation started in 1949 culminated in October 1992 with a husband and wife being convicted at Southwark Crown Court of false accounting. The Hospital Fund Appeal Society had operated, mainly in Kent, selling prize draw tickets from door-to-door, and it was found that only 20 per cent of an annual income of around half a million pounds had gone to hospitals. The Charities Act 1992 obliged professional fundraisers to have a written contract, of an approved form, with the charity employing them; to explain how they were remunerated; and to provide accurate information about that charity when soliciting donations.

Furthermore, their charges could not be disproportionate to the services rendered. Here it had to be remembered that a higher standard of care and diligence was required from professional bodies advertising their services than from any ordinary prudent person who might undertake the work. In 1980, for example, the Barclays Bank Trust Company was ordered to recompense a family trust for losses incurred after imprudent property transactions by the managers of the family property. The court considered that the Trust Company, which had acted as trustee, should have realised the hazards and forbidden the transactions.[85]

There are schemes whereby commercial organisations pass on part of the sale price of their goods to charity. Here it was not always made clear what proportion this represented, and the sum might be much less than the purchaser supposed. Since 1992 these commercial participators are also obliged to have a formal agreement with a charity and to state what part of the purchase price went to that charity. With some goods – Christmas cards for example – the paper work involved in this would be intolerable, as in some circumstances each retailer would need a separate agreement with each charity. With such articles it is preferable to administer the scheme through a central clearing house.

In the past, different laws regulated house to house collections and street collections. This outmoded legislation was swept away and all public collections are now governed by the 1992 Act. A 'public place' was defined and although some members of Parliament wished to exclude such activities as carol singing and 'bob-a-job' weeks, it was decided that this would create anomalies and all collections must be subject to control. Permits had to be obtained from the local authority, who would consult the police, or from the Charity Commission if the collection was nationwide. Conditions might be imposed governing the keeping and publishing of accounts; to prevent annoyance to the public; and to ensure that collectors were of a minimum age and carried badges or letters of authority. Despite the recommendations in the Woodfield Report and the ensuing White Paper, there were criminal sanctions for contravening the requirements of the Act and maximum fines of £2,000 could be imposed.

During the debate on the Charities Bill in the House of Lords, Lord Browne-Wilkinson expressed his worries that the relevant legislation was to be scattered around several Acts, and that 'if the Bill passes into law, those who run charities, their advisers and even, if they may be allowed a moments thought, the judges who have to construe the legislation, will either be forced into a scissors and paste operation, chasing 94 amendments round the Bill, or will have to wait until someone else makes intelligible on a commercial basis what Parliament has not made intelligible'.

The Act of 1993

The Government was sufficiently impressed by this argument to include amended sections of the Charities Act 1960 in Schedule 1 of the 1992 Act. Applying the law still involved constant referral to different pieces of legislation and the Government was finally persuaded that a consolidating Act was necessary. This was the Charities Act 1993,[58] which repealed and consolidated the Charitable Trustees Incorporation Act

1872,[36] the Charities Act 1960,[47] and Part I of the Charities Act 1992.[57] Certain pieces of legislation remained unaffected – notably the Charitable Trust Validation Act 1954, the Recreational Charities Act 1958 and those parts of the Charities Act 1992 which dealt with fundraising.

For many years Quaker families, such as the Gurneys, the Frys, the Hoares and the Cadburys, have played a notable part in charitable activity. The Joseph Rowntree Memorial Trust, for example, still funds housing projects. There are also several very wealthy trusts founded by people of other religious persuasions, including the Rhodes Trust, the Nuffield Foundation, the Isaac Wolfson Foundation and the Wellcome Trust. They seem to have no difficulty in disposing of their considerable funds but the Charity Commission has been concerned about charities with substantial reserves which still continue to raise money as, if such funds are not used to the full, the trustees might be in breach of trust and lose their tax concessions. Here Bridge House Estates, administered by the Corporation of the City of London, was in a particularly difficult position. It had assets of over £300 million, generating an income of over £18 million – far more than was needed to carry out the object of the charity, which was the maintenance and support of London, Blackfriars, Southwark and Tower Bridges. The problem was solved by drawing up a scheme to use the accumulating surplus to provide transport and access for elderly and disabled people in the Greater London area.[86]

In order to bring more fund raising activities under control the relevant provisions of the Charities Act 1992 also applied to a 'charitable institution' which was defined as 'a charity or an institution (other than a charity) which is established for charitable, benevolent or philanthropic purposes'. In its legal sense, a charity has to benefit mankind and it was thought that the term 'charitable institution' would encompass organisations which the court would not consider to confer 'public benefit'. Although both Greenpeace and Amnesty International, for example, are associated with charitable trusts which concentrate on research and the publication of unbiased material, their best-known activities would be judged political, not charitable. Such differences between the popular and legal conceptions of charity have caused confusion, not least to testators and their advisers. As will be seen, what a solicitor to one prominent charity has called 'a somewhat esoteric branch of the law' has even caused members of that unemotional body, the judiciary, to vent their frustration from time to time.

CHAPTER 5

WHAT IS CHARITY ?

Charities and taxation

In the past there were two distinct classes of philanthropic institution: voluntary organisations, usually supported by subscriptions only, and charitable trusts endowed in perpetuity. Charity legislation was intended to prevent abuse of the privileges which charitable trust status conferred – the rights to exist in perpetuity and to have the trust deed amended if it was imprecisely worded or if the stated charitable purpose was unachievable or obsolete. Today there are large voluntary charities with no permanent endowments which raise considerable annual incomes from many donors who each make small subscriptions. Such donors are little concerned with the ancient privileges of charitable trusts but, for the charities themselves, it is most important to be registered with the Charity Commission as this attracts generous fiscal concessions. No general relief from taxation is granted but specific provisions are included in each tax law.

Charities have been exempt from income tax since the first Income Tax Act was introduced by Pitt in 1799 – but not without protest. When Gladstone presented his budget on 16 April 1863 he proposed to remove the exemption, pointing out that it was granted to charitable bequests which did not take effect until after death. In contrast the contributions of the really charitable, whose generosity during life might mean personal privation, were taxed in full. Like eighteenth century lawyers before him, he questioned the encouragement of wills that might leave the testator's family destitute. He also asked if it was right for Parliament to make what were, in effect, grants of money without retaining control over them. There was no serious attempt to refute his arguments but opposition was so widespread that the proposal was withdrawn.

Later the Board of Inland Revenue tried to restrict the exemption to charities founded for the relief of poverty only. The treasurer of the Protestant Episcopal Church protested when his claim for exemption from tax for 1885/6 was refused on the grounds that the income was derived from a gift for missionary work, not the relief of poverty. The gift had been made as long ago as 1812 and, when the case eventually reached the House of Lords in 1891,[71] Lord Macnaghten remonstrated about the refusal of remissions that had been granted for many years. This, he thought, could not be justified by the Board's recent discovery 'that the meaning of charity was not to be ascertained from the legal definition of the expressions actually found in the statute, but to be gathered from the popular use of the word'. The Board lost the case and had to pay costs.

Since then, recognised charities have received tax relief, but often the question of charitable status has first arisen when exemption is sought and, in effect, the Inland Revenue has been the adjudicator. There have been further complications. The case of the Oxford Group,[76] which had subsidiary objects which were not strictly charitable, has already been described. These did not deprive the Group of its status as a charity but it was liable to tax unless the constitution was changed to omit non-charitable objects. In 1953[87] a case was considered in which land had been conveyed to a trust for the erection of a variety of buildings for the Roman Catholic church at Cookstown in Northern Ireland or for use 'generally in such manner for the promotion and aiding of the work of the Roman Catholic Church in the district...as the trustees with the consent of the Bishop may prescribe'. This last general provision was held to enlarge the scope of the trust beyond exclusively charitable purposes. This decision affected a large number of trusts, not only Roman Catholic but also Anglican and Nonconformist also.

47

The Finance Act 1950[43] gave retrospective immunity to such bodies if the offending objects were removed from their constitutions. This dispensation was withdrawn for income tax by the Income Tax Act of 1952[44] and for other taxes by the Finance Act of 1963.[49]

Charities are also exempt from corporation tax. Those registered for VAT can reclaim tax in certain circumstances, and some large charities derive considerable benefit from this concession. Charities are also not liable for the duties payable on bingo games or gaming machines, provided that all the proceeds are devoted to charity. Charities do not have to pay the charges involved in conveying and leasing property. In 1961 and 1967 premises occupied wholly or mainly for charitable purposes were granted large reductions in rates, and religious buildings were exempted altogether. Gladstone would have approved of the tax incentives that now exist for those who give during their lifetime. Tax paid on subscriptions can be reclaimed by charities and a gift to charity is not taken into account when assessing the capital gains tax of the donor.

Attempts to define 'a charity'

Charitable status is not optional. Those who seek it to gain the benefits it confers must also accept supervision by the Charity Commission or some other body. The fiscal concessions substantially reduce the revenues of central and local authorities. In a House of Lords debate, tax relief was said to have amounted to £800 million during 1990/1 and rate relief to £177.5 million during 1989/90. With such sums at stake it was argued that adequate supervision was essential, and also that charitable status should only be granted after rigorous investigation. As far as this is concerned, it would be an advantage to have a clear, comprehensive definition of 'charity', but this has never been exhaustively defined in legislation and the legal concept has gradually evolved from decisions made in the courts.

In 1823, the Master of the Rolls, Sir Thomas Plummer, considered the will of Mr Buckeridge Ball Acworth, who had left considerable legacies of stock to relatives and to several named charities. He had also ordered that his books, jewels and furniture were to be sold 'and in case there is any money remaining, I would wish it to be given in private charity'. Having made separate bequests to 'public charity', the testator had distinguished it from 'private charity' and the court considered that 'assisting individuals in distress is private charity, but how can such a charity be executed by the Court or by the Crown?'. It was ruled that trust deeds containing the term 'private charity' would fail for uncertainty.[88]

To be accepted as charitable a gift must confer public benefit, but in 1805 Lord Eldon conclusively rejected the idea that 'almost everything, from which the public derive benefit, may be considered a charity'.[70] The crux of the argument is that benefit must be conferred on a sufficient section of the public[89] and the Charity Commission will not register a charity unless this is substantiated. Here fine judgment must be required but the following gifts are among those which have been declared void as not being 'pro bono publico': gifts to relatives,[90] staff training colleges, the education of children of employees[91] or of members of a particular profession; and also, the education of the founder's descendants only, although his kin can participate. Friendly societies, trade unions and professional societies are not charitable as they are for mutual, not public, benefit;[92] neither are religious communities interested only in their own salvation, private chapels and Church of England retreat homes.

In addition, of course, the benefit must be of a sort that the law considers charitable. This is still decided by making analogies from past decisions, and the benefit must still

12. **Lord Macnaghten**, by C.L. Hartwell *(reproduced by kind permission of the Benchers of Lincoln's Inn, from a photograph held by the Cortauld Institute of Art).*

be within the spirit of examples listed in the preamble to the Statute of Charitable Uses, passed in 1601[18] which was repealed in 1888. It is hardly surprising that the Victorians and, more recently, lay witnesses to the Nathan Committee were impatient for a more formulated approach. The preamble to the Statute of 1601[18] states how charitable bequests might be used:

> 'some for the relief of aged, impotent and poor People; some for the Maintenance of Sick and Maimed Soldiers and Mariners, Schools of Learning, free Schools and Scholars in Universities, some for the Repair of Bridges, Ports, Havens, Causeways, Churches, Sea-Banks, and Highways; some for the Education and Preferment of Orphans; some for or towards the Relief, Stock or Maintenance for Houses of Correction; some for Marriages of Poor Maids; some for Supportation, Aid and Help of young Tradesmen, Handicraftsmen, and Persons decayed; and others for Relief, Redemption of Prisoners or Captives; and for Aid or Ease of any poor Inhabitants concerning payment of Fifteens, setting out of Soldiers and other Taxes'

Anomalies and the problems of poor drafting

No general definition of charity was attempted, and in 1787 Sir Lloyd Kenyon, the Master of the Rolls, admitted that although the Act of 1601 contained 'a great enumeration of charitable uses...the statute does not affect to mention all'.[93] Before the nineteenth century charitable bequests mostly followed well-worn paths leading to little demand for rigid definitions. Very early in that century a case was considered by the Court of Chancery in which money had been left for 'such objects of benevolence and liberality as the Bishop of Durham in his own discretion, should most approve of'.[70] This case, heard by Lord Eldon, established that 'benevolence and liberality' did not mean 'charitable', a term for which there was no synonym.

In 1889 a will contained the following terms: 'I, John Ross Macduff, will from my estate the sum of 10,000L to be appropriated and allocated for some one or more purposes, charitable, philanthropic or   . The precise purpose or purposes I would desire to be named by my daughter Annie S. Macduff'. It was ruled that the blank was irrelevant, but that the use of the word 'or' indicated that the testator considered 'philanthropic' to differ from 'charitable', and it was unclear what 'philanthropic' meant. It could indicate goodwill to rich men to the exclusion of poor men.[94] More recently terms such as 'most deserving', 'hospitality or charity', 'benevolent purposes', and 'worthy causes' have also been rejected.

Such rulings emphasised the need to be precise when leaving bequests for charity, but sloppy wording continued to be used and, as one judge said in 1941, 'the manifest intentions of various testators seem to me to have been defeated by their artless use of language'.[95] In 1944 there was an outcry over a will made years before, on 3 November 1919.[96] The testator, Caleb Diplock, eventually died on 23 March 1938 leaving no near relatives. Bequests made to certain specified charities were honoured and caused no further trouble. The residue of his estate, amounting to over a quarter of a million pounds, was entrusted to his executors 'for such charitable institution or institutions or other charitable or benevolent object or objects in England as they should in their absolute discretion select'. The executors had already shared this residue among 139 charities when a distant relative challenged the propriety of the distribution. The Court of Chancery ruled that the executors had acted correctly but the case was then taken to appeal and eventually to the House of Lords.

There litigants were reminded that a testator 'cannot leave the disposal of his estate to others' unless the gift was for a charitable purpose and that 'benevolent' did not mean 'charitable', which – as we have seen – had no synonym. It was now ruled that the word 'or' did not mean 'in other words' but separated two alternatives, one of which was not charitable. Lord Simonds pointed out that it was 'true of the law of charity that it has been built up not logically but empirically' and, if 'charitable or benevolent' was allowed, such phrases as 'charitable or philanthropic', and 'charitable or patriotic', would also be permissible. The eventual outcome was that the charities had to return the money for the benefit of a remote relative. Vexation increased when it was realised that if 'or' had been replaced by 'and', the bequest might have been valid.

Doubts can arise from other causes. One testator left £14,000 to Gloucester Corporation and the executors were instructed to give £60,000 more 'for the same purpose as I have before named'. No earlier codicil was found and the House of Lords held that the disposition was void because of uncertainty.[97] However, where a testator leaves property for a particular charitable purpose which is found impossible to execute, as when the named charity does not exist, a *cy-pres* scheme may be drawn up.[98] Although a gift for an illegal purpose certainly fails, the court may presume a general charitable intention if the purpose is charitable though the manner of effecting it is illegal.

If a charity ceases to exist before the testator dies the gift lapses, but if it still exists when the will takes effect the next-of-kin and other beneficiaries are excluded for ever. Should the charity ceases to exist subsequently, the gift is applied *cy-pres*. The British School of Archaeology, founded by Sir Flinders Petrie in 1905, was wound up in 1954, but it was decreed that subscribers had finally parted with their contributions. The Crown waived any claim and the money was used to fund a scholarship in Egyptian Archaeology at University College.[99]

The objects of charity

In 1891[71] Lord Macnaghten said that 'Charity is an elastic notion', as the Act of 1853 setting up the Charity Commission 'contains a definition of "charity" by reference to the Act of Elizabeth, and the practice of the Court of Chancery'. The enumeration of charitable purposes in the Statute of 1601 was 'so varied and comprehensive that it became the practice of the Court to refer to it as a sort of index or chart'. This archaism irritated the Victorians and, in an attempt at improvement, Lord Macnaghten regrouped charitable objects under four headings which were noted in chapter 3:[71]

1 The relief of poverty
2 The advancement of education
3 The advancement of religion
4 Trusts for other purposes beneficial to the community, not falling under one of the preceding heads

Though the lay witnesses to the Nathan Committee were dissatisfied with this definition of 'charity' no new statutory definition was attempted. The legal witnesses thought that dependence on judges' rulings helped to keep decisions in line with current thinking, whereas a statutory definition might ossify the concept of charity. Redefinition would only lead to new 'fringe' areas and it might also overturn existing case law. The committee agreed with the lawyers and suggested a new statute based on Macnaghten's four categories 'but preserving the case law as it stands'.[59] The Government must have thought even this was prejudicial to case law, for though the Mortmain and Charitable Uses Act 1888[38] had abolished the last trace of the preamble to the 1601 Act, Section 45 of the Charities Act 1960[47] left the question of definition

13. Installing a water tank at a camp in Bangladesh for Rohingya refugees from Burma *(reproduced by kind permission of the Photo Library, Oxfam; copyright Howard Davies).*

heavily dependent on the Elizabethan enumeration. Over ten years later, in 1971, Mr Justice Foster found it[100] 'incredible that the law on this subject is still derived from the preamble to the Statute of Elizabeth I, long since repealed and long since out of date, and in modern times applied by analogy upon analogy upon analogy'.

The law had been slow to recognise new charitable purposes and to withdraw recognition from out-of-date trusts, possibly because of the costs of litigation. Furthermore, although such activities had been ruled non-charitable, there was still pressure to use charitable funds for political propaganda. In an attempt to help, the National Council of Social Service (now the National Council for Voluntary Organisations) set up a Committee of Inquiry in 1974, chaired by Lord Goodman,[101] to see if a less archaic definition of 'charity' could be formulated.

This committee was unable to come up with a neat, modern definition but it presented existing categories of charitable uses in simple, modern language as an aid to reaching decisions about charitable status: 'the guidelines are not intended to be either exhaustive or immutable but only to be a statement of the types of activity which at the present time should come properly and eminently within the scope of charitable purposes'. Twenty-six categories were listed, which may have been helpful to the judiciary, but subsequent legislation is still heavily dependent on the enumeration in the statute of 1601[18] and on Lord Macnaghten's classification.[71] If a purpose falls within Macnaghten's fourth category it must be within the spirit and intention of the statute of 1601 or, by the process of analogy, in conformity with some decision in case law.[102]

Purposes excluded from charitable status

There are purposes such as paying fines for imprisoned criminals[103] or promoting revolution in a friendly state[104] that have never been considered charitable, but decisions on other purposes have often depended on contemporary circumstances. After the Reformation 'superstitious uses', uses which had for their objects the propagation of the rites of religions not tolerated by law, were no longer charitable and the 1558 Act of Uniformity[12] excluded all but Anglicanism. Until the late seventeenth century gifts left to the Roman Catholic, Dissenting or Jewish faiths were held void.[21] This situation was gradually alleviated by later laws; the Statute Law (Repeals) Act of 1969[51] repealed the Act of Uniformity and no religion is now proscribed by law. However, saying masses for the dead, the veneration of relics and saints, or providing for the sustenance of miracle workers might still be ruled void, not because they are 'superstitious uses' but rather because they confer no public benefit.

Trusts for the promulgating of a particular point of view, such as educational societies with a trade union character; the Primrose League; a protest against stopping the provision of free milk at schools; the advancement and propagation of socialised medicine;[105] and, more surprisingly, a trust to promote understanding between the Swedish and English peoples have all, at various times, been defined as non-charitable. There have been inconsistent rulings. In 1898, when the vicar of Bishops Itchington left property to his successors 'to be maintained for the furtherance of Conservative principles and religious and mental improvement', Mr Justice Stirling decreed that the gift was charitable as it was for three purposes in combination. The inclusion of the phrase 'Conservative principles' was held merely to place limits on how the religious and mental improvement should be effected.[106] Such a decision would be unlikely to stand today.

The Bonar Law Memorial Trust, set up with £100,000 given to the chairman of the Conservative Party, was intended to honour the memory of a great statesman and to preserve Ashridge House, Hertfordshire, as an educational centre. In 1932 the Commissioners for the Special Purposes of the Income Tax ruled that relief from tax could not be granted as the trust was not charitable. On appeal it was ruled that the main purpose of the trust was to provide a centre 'where those who are disposed to work in the interests of the Conservative Party may go, in order that they may learn what are the principles of the party to which they adhere',[107] and that this was not charitable. As late as 1991 a plaintiff successfully restrained a students' union from using charitable funds to support a campaign against the Gulf War. It was reaffirmed that campaigning to influence public opinion on political matters was not charitable.

Trusts for the attainment of political objectives are considered invalid, not because they are illegal, but because there is no means of judging whether a proposed change in the law will benefit the public. In any case, an object is not charitable if it can be achieved by legislation as this is a matter for Parliament and not the court or the Charity Commissioners.[108] Thus the encouragement of temperance is charitable but not the promotion of legislation to achieve that end.[109] Anti-vivisection societies which seek to have the practice banned are not charitable, not only because of the political activity involved, but also because medical research, beneficial to the public, may be hampered.[110] Nevertheless, the Royal Society for the Prevention of Cruelty to Animals can campaign for legislative changes as 'the existence of some political motive is not necessarily fatal to a good charitable trust' if it is ancillary to the main purpose – which for the R.S.P.C.A. is 'to promote kindness and to prevent or suppress cruelty to animals'. Amnesty International, which aims to change legislation or government policy in this country and abroad, is non-charitable[111]. Just as it is not charitable to press for changes in the law, so any organisation which opposes such changes is also non-charitable.[112]

Residences for public figures are not charitable, as there is no public benefit in providing free housing for the well-to-do. Bearing this in mind, the Chequers Estate Act of 1917[40] was framed to overcome any objections to an estate being left for use by the Prime Minister. In 1954 it was held that a house and land in Bedfordshire left in trust 'for the use of the High Commissioner or other person representing the Government of the Commonwealth of Australia...as a country residence' was not charitable.[113] Despite these limitations new outlets for private generosity are constantly being found. In 1992 a new charity was being registered every thirty minutes of every working day. Purposes that are charitable will now be considered.

CHAPTER 6

CLASSIFICATION OF CHARITABLE PURPOSES

Today charitable purposes are listed under the four heads laid down by Lord Macnaghten in 1891. In the main that grouping will be used here, though where other purposes have become associated with one of the categories they will be discussed together.

1. The relief of poverty

Poverty has drawn the attention of philanthropists for hundreds of years and the 'relief of aged, impotent and poor People' was the first charitable purpose listed in the preamble to the 1601 statute. The three terms have been taken *disjunctively*,[114] which means that it can be charitable to relieve the aged who are not poor, and relief for sick, disabled or other 'impotent' people is charitable even if the recipients are not poor or old.

Unlike all other charitable gifts, those for the poor do not have to confer public benefit. Gifts to relatives, to employees and to their children are all charitable provided that they are restricted to the relief of poverty. Of course gifts to the poor may also be general, but the indiscriminate nature of doles has aroused criticism since Tudor times. Such doles, which were extremely numerous, were not restricted to cash and, for example, in the 1780s at Dent in the West Riding the rent income from three tenements was used to provide poor widows with bread and clothing as well as 2d per week. Handouts of fuel and other necessities were also common. In 1881 a judge considering a dole distributed in Kensington remarked that 'there is no doubt that it tends to demoralise the poor and benefit no one'.[115] The word 'poor' has been taken as a relative term, applying not only to the 'absolutely poor' but also to those who have had a raw deal considering their status, so that the relief of genteel poverty can be charitable. The relief of poverty is sometimes an implied object, as in the provision of local legal aid and advice centres.

The elderly and the young

In 1889 the term 'old' was defined as applying to those aged fifty or over,[116] but this limit would have to be reconsidered today. Almshouses were a time-honoured method of helping the aged poor, but today the provision of homes, or temporary homes of rest, for old people, whether free, subsidised or at an economic rent, is charitable even if the occupants are not poor. Loans for the purchase of accommodation by the aged poor can be charitable but annual reassessments must be carried out to check that the recipients are still necessitous.

Relief for young people is not charitable unless they are considered 'impotent', such as those being cruelly treated. Endowments to provide apprenticeships were really for the relief of poverty and an Act of 1610[19] required that the overseers of the poor must be involved in their distribution. The care of orphans is charitable,[117] as is the provision of homes for children placed in care,[118] but gifts for the benefit of the inmates may not be. As Lord Justice Romer put it, 'I cannot regard the provision of television sets...for the benefit of such children as juvenile delinquents and refractory children...as coming within any conception of charity'.[119]

The sick and the disabled

'Sick and Maimed Soldiers and Mariners' were listed in the preamble to the act of 1601, but the care of the sick and disabled has been generally implied by the use of the term 'impotent'. For hundreds of years health needs were met by the great endowed and voluntary hospitals, in London and elsewhere. Today the National Health Service caters for most needs, though there has been a growth in private hospitals recently. There is some doubt about private medicine benefiting the public, and decisions on hospitals with paying patients have varied. During the nineteenth century such hospitals were ruled non-charitable but on some occasions they have been considered charitable if they do not aim to make a profit.

For example, Edmund Resch died on 2 October 1963 leaving two-thirds of the income from the residue of his estate to be spent on St Vincent's Private Hospital, which was run by Sisters of Mercy. The hospital had eighty-two beds and provided treatment with more privacy than the nearby public hospital which had five hundred beds. The bequest was held to be charitable as the hospital was of public benefit to people of moderate means, and because surpluses paid for the treatment of poor patients or were donated to the public hospital.[120] In 1967 a trust endowing private beds in the Finchley Memorial Hospital was held to be valid.[121] Benefits for hospital staff, such as housing, homes of rest and extra comforts for nurses, are usually considered charitable, as are religious communities for the relief of the poor and sick.

It was particularly important that hospitals nationalised under the National Health Service Act 1946 remained eligible for bequests established before the change in status. Happily, it had already been ruled that if an institution named in a will had been replaced by another with an identical function, the gift could be passed on to the successor. In an 1854 ruling, for example, it was held that 'the sum of 200L to the treasurer of the Benevolent Institution for the delivery of poor married women at their own habitations', which had closed ten years before the death of the testatrix, could be passed to the Royal Maternity Society which performed a similar service.[98] Mrs Fanny Magrath, by her will of 16 February 1910, left £3000 to Queen's College, Belfast where her husband had studied. This college had become part of the Queen's University of Belfast and it was ruled that the gift was valid just as it would have been if there had been a mistake in the name.[122] The work of many bodies such as the District Nursing Associations, started in Liverpool in the 1860s, came to an end when the N.H.S. was set up. Section 23 of the National Health Service (Amendment) Act 1949 empowered local health boards to apply any remaining funds for other purposes but the Charity Commissioners felt obliged to investigate whether some authorities, such as those in Cornwall, had left funds lying idle or transferred them without proper authority.

If the funds left to give effect to a purpose are insufficient the trust fails. Thus, when funds raised between 1924 and 1942 for a new hospital at Ulverston were still inadequate by 1948, when the National Health Service came into operation, the Court of Appeal ruled that the contributions had been made for a specific purpose and they must be returned to the donors, or passed to the Crown when donors could not be traced. The more flexible cy-pres jurisdiction now conferred on the courts and the Charity Commissioners might have proved useful back in 1910. Money was left to found the Weir Hospital and, although it was recognised that it was more efficient and useful to augment a neighbouring hospital, the trustees were given no choice but to carry out the founder's wishes and build a new one.[123]

2. The advancement of education

Education has been accepted as charitable from the time of the Tudor grammar schools and earlier. For many years the Endowed Schools Act 1869[35] placed those schools in a special position, as their trust deeds could be amended with little regard to the trustees or to the original wishes of the founder. Recently similar relaxations have been provided for all charities.

However, not only are gifts for teaching by instruction charitable, but also those for many other educational activities, such as the acquisition and dissemination of knowledge by research, the improvement (but not the mere increase) of a branch of knowledge, and the sponsorship of such cerebral events as chess tournaments. The provision and maintenance of botanic gardens, museums and art galleries is charitable and this can include the objects within them but only if they have educational value.[124] The promotion of art or science by intellectual exercise was considered charitable but only if there was the minimum of enjoyment.

The novelist Marie Corelli wanted the income from her estate to be used to maintain her home, Mason Croft, Stratford-upon-Avon, as a breathing space for the town, as a place for the encouragement of science, literature and music, and 'for the benefit and services of distinguished persons visiting Stratford-upon-Avon from far countries'.[125] It was decided that either of the first two purposes was charitable but that the third was not and, as this was considered the dominant purpose, the trust was declared void. Some gifts for vocational, professional, scientific or commercial training are charitable and these include those for training clergy, lawyers, nurses and surgeons. Education and training in particular subjects (such as drama or Egyptology) are charitable, and so is the education of a limited class, such as employees in the whole of a particular industry. Bodies formed for mental improvement, such as the Royal Society, and for moral and physical improvement, such as the Scouts, are charitable.

Gifts for the foundation and support of colleges, for scholarships, for students' unions, for the promotion of organised games and for the provision of sporting facilities, are all charitable. To be valid a trust does not have to be confined to the education of the poor and, like hospitals, fee-paying schools can be charitable if they are not profit-making ventures.[126]

The problem of aesthetics

The nurturing of public taste in aesthetic matters is charitable but, in this area, decisions are difficult to reach. The presentation of plays and the production of books are charitable, but only if they have 'merit'. Shows of 'masterpieces' are charitable, but not those of any old pictures! In 1961, for example, money had been left to fund the display of a testator's considerable collection of paintings, furniture and bric-a-brac. They had been offered to the National Trust who declined them and one of the experts asked to evaluate the collection expressed his surprise: 'I would have expected that a person with the testator's voracious appetite for bric-a-brac would occasionally have acquired some pieces of mediocre quality, but that has not proved to be the case'.[124] Lord Justice Russell declared for an intestacy, making the bequest void.

Music societies can be charitable only if they were not primarily for the amusement of the members. A harmonic society was held to be not charitable in 1884 because it existed only for the members' diversion and was not educational. In 1929 David King left gifts to a Barnado's Home, to relieve the poor and sick, and to help promising youngsters. These gifts were considered charitable but others, for the promotion of sports and games and of literary and musical societies were not.[127] On the other hand, the Royal Choral Society was considered charitable as it had no profit motive and promoted aesthetic education.[128]

3. The advancement of religion

The promotion of a religious message, and the sustaining and encouragement of religious belief is perhaps the most ancient charitable purpose, but it has had a chequered history. Before the Reformation, gifts for religious purposes might be used, not only for the direct benefit of the Church, but also to relieve the poor or for public works. After the Reformation gifts for 'superstitious uses' were not charitable but, since the revoking of the Act of Uniformity by the Statute Law (Repeals) Act of 1969[51] no religion has been prescribed by law. The Charity Commission has therefore registered Hindu, Sikh, Islamic, and Buddhist charities.

But gifts to religious societies are not always charitable.[129] Nowadays, doctrines must be for the edification and instruction of the public, so contemplative or secluded orders are excluded. In one case, Evelyn Dudley Coats had left £500 to a Carmelite Priory in Notting Hill, provided that its purposes were charitable. When the House of Lords considered this in 1949 it was represented that the Roman Catholic Church held that the contemplative life of a religious community conferred benefits, not only on the community, but also on the public through the efficacy of intercessory prayers and through edification by example. The lord chancellor, Lord Simonds, felt that 'it does not follow from this that the courts must accept as proved whatever a particular church believes. The faithful must embrace their faith believing where they cannot prove: the court can act only on proof'.[130] The priory was therefore held to be non-charitable.

Religious orders can be considered charitable if they are socially active. Frances Manners, who died in 1870, left funds for two religious institutions near Birmingham, one seeking personal sanctification for its members by teaching poor children and tending the sick, the other by religious exercises and self-denial. The first was held to be charitable but the second was not, particularly as its religious services did not tend 'directly or indirectly' towards the instruction or the edification of the public'.[131] The social work of the Society of Precious Blood, a contemplative order, was held to be sufficiently public as it was carried out by outside workers whose activities were well publicised, but in 1989 the Charity Commission recommended that its constitution should be amended to emphasise the extent of this work.[132]

Limitations on support for religion

Although there is now no distinction between sects and even a purpose contrary to ecclesiastical law[133] is not invalid, there are still some restrictions. To be recognised as charitable, faiths must not offend public morality, or promote pernicious knowledge, or contravene public policy. There is some ambiguity about 'missionary purposes' which may comprise objects that are not charitable. In 1949 the Oxford Group[76] was held to have secular, as well as religious, aims and, as it had no formal constitution, a gift was declared invalid for uncertainty.

Support of the clergy, holders of religious offices, of religious buildings and of burial grounds are charitable. In 1935 a testatrix[134] left $10,000 [sic] to a Chiswick church to maintain the burial ground and a monument to her husband and herself and for church purposes. It was held to be a gift for the maintenance of the church and the churchyard, which is charitable, whereas monuments and tombs, which do not form an integral part of the fabric, are not valid as objects of charity.

It is charitable to help and protect minorities,[135] to promote good race relations and to eliminate discrimination. Trust deeds can be affected by the Race Relations Act 1976[53] as any stipulation that benefits must go to people of a particular colour will be disregarded. In contrast, benefits conferred on one sex only are unaffected by the Sex Discrimination Act 1975[52] with one exception. That exception is for education, where the restriction may be removed.

Trustees should not over-emphasise their beliefs when investing trust property. In 1991 it was held that the purpose of a trust was best served by maximising the return from investments. Though these investments should not bring the charity into disrepute there should be no attempt to make moral statements on which the trustees may disagree anyway.[136]

4. Other purposes beneficial to the community

Lord Macnaghten listed as his fourth, portmanteau, category, 'trusts for other purposes beneficial to the community, not falling under one of the preceding heads'. Additional purposes, not considered as charitable in his day, have now been included in this group. Purposes in this category must benefit the community,[137] and be of practical utility.[138]

Animals and their welfare

The British pride themselves on their care and concern for animals. In 1923, the Master of the Rolls, Lord Sterndale, commented: 'I confess I find considerable difficulty in understanding the exact reason why a gift for the benefit of animals...should be a good charitable gift, while a gift for philanthropic purposes, which, I take it, is for the benefit of mankind generally, should be bad as a charitable gift'.[139] Despite this, animal charities must confer 'public benefit', which implies that they must be of use to man – if only for his moral elevation. Francesca Wedgwood left funds for the humane slaughter of animals which was considered a charitable purpose as 'Cruelty is degrading to man; and...the suppression of cruelty to the lower animals...has for its object, not merely the protection of animals, but the advancement of morals and education among men'.[140]

On the other hand, when Mrs Grove-Grady left the residue of her estate to acquire land for animal refuges to which people would not have access, the trust was held to be void as it was of no benefit to the community. The Master of the Rolls, Lord Hanworth declared wryly that 'The one characteristic of the refuge is that it is free from the molestation of man, while all the fauna within it are to be free to molest and harry one another'.[141] Research into methods of substituting animals in experiments is charitable.[142]

In an 1889 case it was agreed that an annuity of £750 left by William Clapcott Dean to care for his horses and hounds should be paid but it was pointed out that an animal cannot enforce a trust and, as it was not for the benefit of animals generally, it was not charitable. So it was not perpetual and the benefits would revert to the heir when the animals had died.[143] Vegetarian societies have been adjudged charitable, though somewhat grudgingly. In 1905 a society for 'furtherance of the principles of food reform as advocated by the vegetarian societies of Manchester and London' was considered. Although the judges thought any public benefit was improbable, they were prepared to defer to the testator's sincere beliefs.[144]

Public works and economic projects

Today most public works are the responsibility of statutory authorities and utilities, but in the past schemes as varied as those for bringing spring water to Chepstow (1767), sea protection at Brighton (1818) and providing a fire brigade at Wokingham (1951) have been considered charitable. As always, the trust deed must be worded with care: a gift for 'charity or works of public utility' was held to be void. As recently as 1981 the Charity Commissioners registered a trust to provide a statue of Earl Mountbatten 'as likely to foster patriotism and good citizenship and to be an incentive to heroic and noble deeds'.

The promotion of an economic activity, such as agriculture,[145] can be considered charitable. In 1914 the Crystal Palace Trustees were set up to acquire the palace and grounds. As the scheme was intended to make the land available for public resort and the 'promotion of industry, commerce and art'[146] it was held to be charitable, as was the Clerkenwell Green Association for Craftsmen – because 'craftsmanship in general is an activity which is of utility to the public'.[147]

Gifts to the fighting forces and the police can be charitable. In 1905, for example, a gift to 'promote the defence of the United Kingdom' was upheld.[148] Benefits for ex-servicemen are charitable but not the provision of houses for former officers. Trusts for promoting the efficiency of the police and the preservation of public order would be charitable, but in one case a gift was held to be not charitable as it was not for those purposes exclusively but was mainly recreational.[149]

Specified parishes, towns and counties have been named in bequests, and these have been held to be charitable provided that they confer public benefit. Thus a gift to preserve an oyster fishery at Saltash has been held charitable,[150] as has a gift of land to be used as a turf common by local inhabitants.[151] The relief of distress after a disaster is charitable, but here difficulties can be caused if a public appeal is oversubscribed. The donors in such cases can rarely be identified and therefore their money cannot be returned. After the Lynton and Lynmouth floods in 1952 over £1.25 million was collected for the North Devon and West Somerset Relief Fund.[152] All claims had been disposed of by 1959 and the Charity Commissioners made a *cy-pres* scheme authorising the expenditure of the surplus of £250,000 on other charitable projects in the area. In a recent pamphlet (CC40) the Charity Commissioners advise that public appeals should make it clear what is the purpose of the appeal, who the beneficiaries will be and how any surplus will be used.

Instruction, not enjoyment

Enjoyment played no part in charity until the passage of the Recreational Charities Act in 1958.[46] Before then, to be considered as charitable, the deeds of trusts for the promotion of music, art and science had to emphasise the educational and intellectual benefits, and certainly not the pleasure, to be obtained from such activities! Gifts merely to promote a sport – for example, angling[153] or hunting[154] – were not considered charitable whereas the provision of community centres or Boy Scout huts was. All this changed with the 1958 Act, which stated that 'it shall be and be deemed always to have been charitable to provide, or assist in the provision of, facilities for recreation or other leisure-time occupations, if the facilities are provided in the interests of social welfare'. This was stated to cover the provision of facilities for those who could not be expected to provide them for themselves: the old, the young, those who were handicapped, sick or disabled and those unfortunately located, such as sailors in a foreign port.

Public benefit had still to be conferred and past court decisions were not overruled. Despite this relaxed attitude, sports clubs may still run into difficulty. In 1989, it was decided that the dominant purpose of an athletic club, the Birchfield Harriers, was to encourage competition and not to improve health or education. Furthermore, as membership of another club precluded membership of Birchfield Harriers, the club could hardly be considered to confer public benefit.[155]

5. Charities operating overseas

In 1852 Dickens had little time for Mrs Jellyby who, oblivious to the misery around her, 'could see nothing nearer than Africa'. Nowadays, when many of our own social needs are met by the state, distress overseas has provided a growing outlet for private generosity and the activities of charities such as Oxfam and War on Want are expanding rapidly. Such charities have the usual difficulties of raising funds and ensuring that those funds are properly applied. They must also be particularly careful not to prejudice their charitable status and, as the annual report of the Charity Commissioners for 1963 made clear, this is by no means straightforward. The commissioners had no doubt that the advancement of religion and of education were charitable purposes in any part of the world, as was the relief of poverty, but overseas charities must ensure that poverty 'actually exists in observable cases and is not merely inferred from statistics' and that measures to relieve it, such as irrigation schemes, 'will have a reasonably direct result'.

14. **A rescue at sea by a crew of the Royal National Lifeboat Institution.** The R.N.L.I. has demonstrated what can be achieved by volunteers - since it was founded in 1824 its unpaid crews have saved over 125,000 lives (*reproduced by kind permission of the Royal National Lifeboat Institution*).

Purposes falling within Macnaghten's fourth group will only be charitable if they benefit the community of the United Kingdom. This benefit need not be material or direct, and charities with general humanitarian objects, such as research into disease, could benefit this country even if they were carried out abroad. The charitable status of public works or development projects carried out in another country depends upon a number of factors. If they relieved existing poverty directly they were charitable, but if they were intended for the general economic improvement of the country they were not. Even here, however, it might be charitable to promote the general benefit of Commonwealth countries emerging from dependent to sovereign status.[156]

Charities which operate entirely abroad come under the jurisdiction of foreign courts. For immovable property, they are governed by the laws of the country where the property is situated,[157] and for movable property by the laws of the country where the testator died.[158] In the late 1970s several overseas charities might have become involved in political agitation. War on Want, wishing to move from traditional forms of relief to overcoming causes of poverty, produced a journal *Poverty and Power* and Oxfam published an article on land reform in the Third World. The Charity Commission had to advise them that they were in danger of impairing their charitable status.[108] Even for charities based within the communities they serve, it is by no means easy to discover what beneficiaries really need. How much harder this must be for charities operating overseas.

Conclusion

In a recent Parliamentary debate Lord Houghton said there were three growth industries in Britain: crime, charity and borrowing money. In this country the greatest of these is undoubtedly charity, where we have a proud tradition. The Nathan Committee[59] described past attempts to provide comprehensive welfare services, entirely on a voluntary basis, as 'one of the magnificent failures of our history'. Today our charities still play a vital role, supplementing official welfare services and giving relief where there is no statutory provision. Recently they have provided massive aid to those less fortunate citizens of countries where 'social security' is unknown. In 1992 there were over 170,000 registered charities with an estimated turnover of £17 billion. To supervise such vast resources some element of professional management is essential, especially now the Charities Act 1992 has moved management responsibility back to the trustees.

Yet, writing in 1992, two professional lawyers, Fiona Middleton & Stephen Lloyd, pleaded that, voluntary workers, the original mainspring of charity, should not be discouraged: 'it is a truism to say that the voluntary sector must remain voluntary. To do so it must encourage those citizens who lack confidence, and those who may not by some be thought particularly 'capable', to be volunteers'. As the role and cost of the 'welfare state' are challenged, it is likely that charity will play an increasingly active role in many aspects of society. This will be difficult to achieve if charity becomes a specialist activity, remote from the hopes, the sympathies, the involvement of ordinary people. But charity has been in existence for thousands of years, and perhaps remains a basic human instinct – its long history suggests that charity will be able to cope with fresh and varied demands, and to carry out a key role in the future.

SOURCE MATERIAL

For those interested in a particular charity the obvious starting point is the charity itself, which may hold its own archives or knows where they are deposited. There may be insufficient information to approach the charity direct, and in such cases the Central Register held at the Charity Commission can be invaluable. This holds details of over 170,000 current registered charities, including full titles, charitable objectives and names of people to contact. The register has been transferred to a database and enquiries about registered charities can be made using computer terminals at any of the three offices listed below:

London St Alban's House, 57/60 Haymarket, SW1Y 4QX
Tel: 0171 210 4405/4533/4685
Hours: 10 am - 4 pm

Liverpool Graeme House, Derby Square, Liverpool, L2 7SB
Tel: 0151 227 3191 Extns 2461/2210
Hours: 9.30 am - 4 pm

Taunton Woodfield House, Tangier, Taunton, TA1 4BL
Tel: 01823 345030
Hours: 9.30 am - 4 pm

Charities can be traced using registration numbers, full or partial names, locations or objectives. Files holding reports and accounts, governing documents and a register of persons removed as trustees are also available but here prior notice must be given as the files may not be held on site. Each office is responsible for a different geographical area and specialises in particular aspects of charitable administration. These are set out in a free leaflet (CC45) published by the Commissioners, which also lists the services available and any charges payable.

The Commission also has information about charities that have ceased to exist. Early reports of the Commissioners contain details of ancient charities then under investigation. Also there is a full set of the reports of the Brougham Commission which investigated many thousands of charities operating in the first half of the nineteenth century. There is comprehensive documentation about charitable legislation, particularly of that enacted since 1853 when the Commission was founded. This includes reports of preparatory committees and commissions, of Parliamentary debates, the acts themselves and subsequent commentaries on them. The legal concept of charity is largely based on court decisions and there are full sets of law reports.

The House of Lords Record Office has information about charitable legislation before 1853 and the parliamentary papers contain much about educational charities. The *Abstract of the Answers and Returns Relative to the Poor* (1803-4) shows the number of children in schools of industry and describes the state of the parochial schools. A Select Committee on the Education of the Lower Orders produced reports in 1817 and 1818 and a *Digest of Parochial Returns* in 1819. The Schools Enquiry Commission of 1868-9 (the Taunton Commission and the Royal Commission on Secondary Education of 1895 (the Bryce Commission) both issued reports giving information about grammar and other schools offering secondary education.

Records of dealings between charities and government departments will be held at the Public Record Office (Kew) but some of these cannot be made public until long periods have elapsed, medical records and reports of school inspectors for example.

The PRO also has the Chantry Certificates of 1546 and 1548 resulting from acts of 1545 (37 Hen VIII, c4) and 1547 (1 Edw VI, c 14) which set up Commissioners to find out about charities and their founders; also the proceedings of the Elizabethan Commissioners for Charitable Uses. Files about endowed schools covering the period 1850 to 1903 include reports and correspondence of the Endowed Schools Commission and the Charity Commission which succeeded to the responsibilities in 1874.

The Guildhall Library has information on charities administered by the Corporation of London and by the Liveried Companies though some Liveried Companies still maintain their own libraries.

Some of the earliest charity schools were founded by the Society for Propagating Christian Knowledge and their archives are held at Holy Trinity Church, Marylebone Road, London, NW1 4DU. In the nineteenth century many elementary Anglican schools were founded by the National Society for Promoting Religious Education and its records are now at Church House, Great Smith Street, Westminster, London, SW1P 3NZ. Non-denominational schools were founded by the British and Foreign School Society which is now based at Eden Street, Kingston upon Thames, KT1 1HZ. Reports of the Catholic Poor School Committee for 1847 and later years are held at the British Library.

During the latter half of the nineteenth century many voluntary (non-endowed) charities were investigated by the Charity Organisation Society (C.O.S.). Reports of these investigations, and correspondence with charities, are held at the Greater London Record Office but permission to view them must be obtained from the Family Welfare Association at 501-505 Kingsland Road, Dalston, London, E8 4AU (Tel: 0171 254 6251). Books and documents from the C.O.S. library are now held in the Goldsmith's Library at Senate House, University of London. These include material about some of the fraudulent 'charities' operating during the late nineteenth and early twentieth centuries. Another possible source of information is the National Council for Voluntary Organisations at 26 Bedford Square.

The most likely source for information about local charities is the county or district record office, as many charities have deposited records in these repositories. Furthermore, a great deal of material about countless local parochial charities is now including within the collections of parish records kept in record offices. It is worth checking in advance what the office holds, and also finding out whether there are any published histories of local or regional charities. Many older schools, for example, now have their own histories and these may be based on charity records, while some charities have also been the subject of books and papers.

They may also hold a copy of the Brougham Report for the county, or other printed material. The printed reports of the Municipal Corporations Commissioners in 1834-5 often include details of urban charities. Information about the proceedings of the Elizabethan commissioners and later investigations and details of local and national statutes and regulations affecting charities in the county may be available in printed or manuscript form at the library or record office. Most volumes of the *Victoria History of the Counties of England* contain a section on charities and the relevant volume should be available in many libraries. Halsbury's *Laws of England and Wales* (Volume 5(2) deals with current charitable legislation). The local studies library is another important place to consider.

Published local histories of individual communities may well deal with charities – with varying degrees of accuracy and reliability: beware of 'antiquarian' histories which simply list those charities which nominally existed, and give no information or analysis about their actual effectiveness or whether they even functioned. There is an enormous range of published social and economic history with reference to charities, often in passing. If the particular charity which is being researched had a specific aim – housing, education, or the provision of a hospital, for example – it is very important to consider the wider context and to see how the general history of the subject bears upon the local example.

REFERENCES

Statutes

1	9 Henry 3 c36	Magna Carta 1225
	7 Edw 1 St 2	Statute of Mortmain 1281
	13 Edw 1 c32	Statute of Westminster 1287
	18 Edw 3 St 3 c3	Statute of the Clergy 1345
	15 Ric 2 c5	Statute of Mortmain 1391
2	15 Ric 2 c6	Appropriation of Benefices 1391
3	4 Hen 4 c12	Enforcement of 1391 Statute 1402
4	2 Hen 5 c1	Government of Hospitals 1414
5	23 Hen 8 c10	Property left to the Church 1532
6	25 Hen 8 c20	Against payment of first fruits to the Bishop of Rome 1534
7	27 Hen 8 c10	Statute of Uses 1535
8	27 Hen 8 c25	Against Vagabonds and Beggars 1535
9	37 Hen 8 c4	Dissolution of Chantries 1545
10	1 Edw 6 c14	Dissolution of Chantries 1547
11	5 & 6 Edw 6 c2	Relief of the poor 1551
12	1 Eliz 1 c2	Act of Uniformity 1558
13	14 Eliz 1 c5	Punishment of Vagabonds and Relief of the Poor 1572
14	14 Eliz 1 c14	Hospitals for the poor 1572
15	39 Eliz 1 c3	Poor Law 1597
16	39 Eliz 1 c5	Hospitals and Workhouses for Poor 1597
17	39 Eliz 1 c6	Reform of Charitable Trusts 1597
18	43 Eliz 1 c4	Statute of Charitable Uses 1601
19	7 Jac 1 c3	Statute of Apprentices 1610
20	29 Car 1 2 c3	Statute of Frauds 1677
21	1 Will & M c18	Toleration Act 1689
22	9 Geo 2 c36	Mortmain Act 1736
23	26 Geo 3 c58	Charitable Donations Returns 1786
24	52 Geo 3 c101	Romilly's Act 1812
25	52 Geo 3 c102	Registration of Charities 1812
26	58 Geo 3 c91	Brougham Commission 1818
27	59 Geo 3 c81	Charitable Foundations 1819
28	10 Geo 4 c7	Roman Catholic Relief 1829
29	7 Will IV & 1 Vic c26	Statute of Wills 1837
30	3 & 4 Vic c77	Grammar Schools 1840
31	16 & 17 Vic c137	Charitable Trusts 1853
32	17 & 18 Vic c100	Court of Chancery 1854
33	18 & 19 Vic c124	Charitable Trusts Amendment 1855
34	23 & 24 Vic c136	Charitable Trusts 1860
35	32 & 33 Vic c56	Endowed Schools 1869
36	35 & 36 Vic c24	Charitable Trustees Incorporation 1872
37	46 & 47 Vic c36	City of London Parochial Charities 1883
38	51 & 52 Vic c42	Mortmain and Charitable Uses 1888
39	54 & 55 Vic c73	Mortmain and Charitable Uses 1891
40	7 & 8 Geo 5 c55	Chequers Estate 1917
41	15 & 16 Geo 5 c19	Trustees 1925
42	3 & 4 Geo 6 c31	War Charities 1940
43	14 Geo 6 c15	Finance 1950
44	15 & 16 Geo 6 & 1 Eliz 2 c33	Finance 1952
45	2 & 3 Eliz 2 c58	Charitable Trusts 1954
46	6 & 7 Eliz 2 c17	Recreational Charities 1958
47	8 & 9 Eliz 2 c58	Charities 1960
48	9 & 10 Eliz 2 c62	Trustees Investment 1961
49	11 & 12 Eliz 2 c25	Finance 1963
50	(1964) Eliz 2 c55	Perpetuities and Accumulation
51	(1969) Eliz 2 c52	Statute Law (Repeals)
52	(1975) Eliz 2 c65	Sex Discrimination
53	(1976) Eliz 2 c74	Race Relations
54	(1981) Eliz 2 c54	Supreme Court
55	(1985) Eliz 2 c20	Charities
56	(1987) Eliz 2 c15	Reverter of Sites
57	(1992) Eliz 2 c41	Charities [1992]
58	(1993) Eliz 2 c10	Charities [1993]

References

59 *Report of the Committee on the Law and Practice relating to Charitable Trusts* (1952) [Nathan Report]

60 Harleian MS 6886 f.228 in British Library (contains Coke's report on Finch v Throgmorton)

61 Croft v Jane Evetts (1606), Moore K.B. 784

62 Hale MS LXXXII no 8 at Lincoln's Inn

63 Emmanuel College, Cambridge v English (1617), cases temp. Bacon, 27,28

64 Thomas More, *Utopia* (1531) (trans. R. Robinson, Everyman's Library edition: Dent 1978, pp 26, 29, 33)

65 Attorney-General v Whiteley (1805), 11 Ves 241, 251

66 Parliamentary Debates (Hansard), XXXVIII, 1230 (1818)

67 Coventry Corporation v A-G (1720) 7 Bro Parl Cas 235, HL

68 Attorney-General v Pearson (1835) 7 Sim 29 Vat 309

69 *Annual Report of the Charitable Organisation Society* 1877

70 Morice v Bishop of Durham (1804) 9 Ves 399, (1805) 10 Ves 522

71 Commissioners for Special Purposes of the Income Tax v Pemsel [1891] AC 531, 581

72 Attorney-General v Ironmongers' Company (1840), 2 Beav.313, (1844), 10Cl & F.908

73 re Knox, Fleming v Carmichael [1937] Ch 109

74 re Dominican Students' Hall Trust Ch 183

75 re Good's Will Trusts, Oliver v Batten [1950] 2 All ER 653

76   Oxford Group v Inland Revenue Commissioners [1949] 2 All ER 537; 93 SJ 525; 31 TC 221; [1949] WN 37

77   re Mead's Trust Deed, Briginshaw v National Society of Operative Printers and Assistants [1961] 2 All ER 836 [1961] 1 WLR 1244

78   re Gillingham Bus Disaster Fund [1959] Ch 62

79   re Hampton Fuel Allotment Charity [1989] Ch 484

80   sub nom Richmond upon Thames London Borough Council v Rogers [1988] 2 All ER 761, CA

81   Gibson v South American Stores (Gath & Chaves) Ltd [1950] Ch 177, [1949] 2 All ER 985, CA

82   re Cooper's Conveyance Trusts, Crewdson v Bagot [1956] 3 All ER 28, [1956] 1 WLR 1096

83   re Woodhams, Lloyds Bank Ltd v London College of Music [1981] 1 All ER202

84   P. Woodfield, G. Binns, R. Hirst and D. Neal [Woodfield Committee], *Efficiency Scrutiny of the Supervision of Charities: Report to the Home Secretary and the Economic Secretary to the Treasury* (1987)

85   Bartlett and Others v Barclays Bank Trust Co Ltd [1980] Ch 515

86   *Annual Report of the Charity Commissioners for England and Wales* (19920

87   Trustees of Cookstown Roman Catholic Church v Inland Revenue Commissioners (1953) 34 TC 350

88   Ommanney v Butcher (1823) Turn and R 260

89   Verge v Somerville [1924] AC 496 at 499, PC

90   Attorney-General v Duke of Northumberland (1877) 7m Ch D 745

91   Oppenheim v Tobacco Securities Trust Co Ltd [1951] AC 297 [1951] 1 All ER 31, HL

92   Geologists Association v Inland Revenue Commissioners (1928) 14 TC 271

93   Turner v Ogden (1787) 1 Cox, 316,317

94   re Macduff, Macduff v Macduff [1896] 2 Ch 451, CA

95   re Ward, Public Trustee v Ward [1941] Ch 308, CA

96   Chichester Diocesan Fund & Board of Finance Inc v Simpson [1944] 2 All ER 60 [1944] AC 341, HL

97   Gloucester Corporation v Osborn (1847), 1 HL Cas 272

98   Coldwell v Holme (1854) 2 Sm & G 31

99   re British School of Egyptian Archaeology, Murray v Public Trustee [1954] 1 All ER 887, [1954] 1 WLR 546

100 Incorporated Council of Law Reporting for England and Wales v Attorney-General [1971] Ch 626 [1971] 1 All ER 436

101 *Charity Law and Voluntary Organisations: Report of the Goodman Committee* (1976) [set up in September 1974 by the National Council of Social Service]

102 Scottish Burial Reform and Cremation Society Ltd v Glasgow City Corporation [1968] AC 138, [1967] 3 All ER 215, HL

103 Thrupp v Collett (1858) 23 Beav 125

104 Habershon v Vardon (1851) 4 De G & Sm 467

105 re Bushnell, Lloyds Bank Ltd v Murray [1975] 1 All ER 721, [1975] 1 WLR 1596

106 re Scowcroft, Ormrod v Wilkinson (1898) 2 Ch 638

107 Bonar Law Memorial Trust v Inland Revenue Commissioners [1933] 49 TLR 220

108 *Annual Reports of the Charity Commissioners for England and Wales:* 1969 (pp 5-6), 1978 (pp 11-13) and 1981 (pp 22-23)

109 Inland Revenue Commissioners v Temperance Council of Christian Churches of England and Wales [1926] 10 Tax Case 748

110 National Anti-Vivisection Society v Inland Revenue Commissioners [1948] AC 31

111 McGovern v Attorney General [1982] Ch 321

112 re Koeppler Will Trusts, Barclays Bank Trust Co Ltd v Slack [1984] Ch 423

113 re Spensley's Will Trusts, Barclays Bank Ltd v Staughton [1954] Ch 233 [1954] 1 All ER 178, CA

114 re Glyn's Will Trusts, Public Trustee v Attorney-General [1950] 2 All ER 1150n

115 re Campden Charities (1881) 18 ChD 310,50 LJCh 646, 45 LT 152, 30 WR 496, CA

116 re Wall, Pomeroy v Willway (1889) 42 Ch D 510

117 Harbin v Masterman [1894] 2 Ch 184, CA

118 re Sahal's Will Trusts, Alliance Insurance Co Ltd v Attorney-General [1958] 3 All ER 428, [1958] 1 WLR 1243

119 re Cole, Westminster Bank Ltd v Moore [1958] Ch 877, [1958] 3 All ER 102, CA

120 re Resch's Will Trusts, Le Cras v Perpetual Trustee Co Ltd [1969] 1 ac 514 [1967] 3 All ER 915, PC

121 Gee & Another v Barnet Group Hospital Management Committee & Others [1967] 3 All ER 285

122 re Magrath, Histed v Queen's University of Belfast [1913] 2 Ch 331

123 re Weir Hospital [1910] 2 Ch 124, 79 LJ Ch 725, 102 LT 882, 26 TLR 519, CA

124 re Pinion, Westminster Bank Ltd v Pinion [1965] Ch 85 [1964]

125 re Corelli, Watt v Bridges, [1943] Ch 332

126 Abbey Malvern Wills Ltd v Ministry of Local Government and Planning [1951] Ch 728

127 re King, Henderson v Cranmer [1931] WN 232

128 Royal Choral Society v IRC [1943] 2 All ER 101

129 re White, White v White (1893) 2 Ch 41, CA

130 Gilmour v Coats [1949] AC 426, [1949] 1 All ER 848, EL

131 Cocks v Manners (1871) LR 12 Eq 574, 40 LJCh 640, 24 LT 8969, 36 JP 244, 19 WR 1055

132 *Annual Report of the Charity Commissioners for England and Wales,* 1989

133 Bowman v Secular Society Ltd [1917] AC 406. HL

134 re Eighmie, Colbourne v Wilks [1935] Ch 524

135 Londonderry Presbyterian Church House Trustees v IRC [1946] NI 178,CA

136 *Annual Report of the Charity Commissioners for England and Wales,* 1983

137 Williams' Trustees v IRC [1947] AC 447, [1947] 1 All ER 513

138 Attorney-General v Governors of Harrow School (1754) 2 Ves Sen 551

139 re Tetley [1923] 1 Ch. 258, 266-7

140 re Wedgwood, Allen v Wedgwood [1915] 1 Ch 113, CA

141 Attorney-General v Plowden [1931] WN 89. HL
142 re Green's Will Trusts, Fitzgerald-Hart v Attorney-General [1985] 3 All ER 445
143 re Dean, Cooper-Dean v Stevens (1889), 41 Ch D 552
144 re Slatter, Howard v Lewis [1905], 21 TLR 295
145 Inland Revenue Commissioners v Yorkshire Agricultural Society [1928] 1 KB 611
146 Crystal Palace Trustees v Ministry of Town and Country Planning [1951] Ch 132
147 Inland Revenue Commissioners v White and Attorney-General [1980] 55 TC 651
148 re Good, Harington v Watts [1905] 2 Ch 60
149 Inland Revenue Commissioners v City of Glasgow Police Athletic Association [1953] AC 380 [1953] 1 All ER 747, HL
150 Goodman v Saltash Corporation (1882) 7 App Cas 633, HL
151 re Christchurch Enclosure Act (1888) 38 Ch D 520
152 re North Devon and Somerset Relief Fund Trusts, Baron Hyelon v Wright [1953] 2 All ER 1032 (1953) 1 WLR 1260)
153 re Clifford, Mallam v McFie [1912] 1 Ch 29, 81 LJCh 220
154 Peterborough Royal Foxhound Show Society v IRC [1936] 2 KB 497, [1936] 1 All ER 813
155 *Annual Report of the Charity Commissioners for England and Wales*, 1989
156 *Annual Report of the Charity Commissioners for England and Wales*, 1963
157 Philipson-Stow v IRC [1961] AC 727, [1960] 3 All ER 814, HL
158 re Levick's Will Trusts, ffenell v IRC [1963] 1 All ER 95, [1963] 1 WLR 311

BIBLIOGRAPHY

This bibliography includes the sources used in the preparation of the present volume, and also a very selective range of other books and articles. The latter have been included to illustrate the type of material which is readily available in published form: examples for particular areas and places can readily be found from local history libraries.

N. ALVEY, 'The great voting charities of the metropolis', in The Local Historian vol.21 no.4 (Nov 1991), pp.147-55

N. ALVEY, 'The Royal Hospital and Home, Putney', in The Local Historian vol.24 no.1 (Feb 1994), pp.15-27

A. BRIGGS, A Social History of England (Weidenfeld and Nicolson 1983)

A.G. CROSBY (ed), The Family Records of Benjamin Shaw (Record Society of Lancashire & Cheshire, vol 130 1991)

E. GREEN, 'Charity schools in the London Borough of Bromley', in The Local Historian vol.24 no.3 (Aug 1994), pp.145-52

J. HACKNEY, Understanding Equity and Trusts (Fontana 1987)
Halsbury's Laws of England and Wales, Vol 5(2) (Butterworths 1993)

J.S. HART, Justice upon Petition: the House of Lords and the Reformation of Justice 1621-1675 (Harper-Collins 1991)

C.P. HILL, A Guide for Charity Trustees (Faber 1974)

G. JONES, History of the Law of Charity 1532- 1827 (Cambridge UP 1969)

M.G. JONES, The Charity School Movement, a Study of Eighteenth Century Puritanism in Action (Cambridge UP 1938)

W.K. JORDAN, The Charities of London 1480- 1660 (George Allen & Unwin 1960)

W.K. JORDAN, The Social Institutions of Lancashire: a study of the changing patterns of aspirations in Lancashire 1480-1660 (Chetham Society 3rd ser. vol. 11, 1962)

W.K. JORDAN, The Charities of Rural England 1480-1660 (George Allen & Unwin 1961)

W.K. JORDAN, Philanthropy in England 1480-1660 (George Allen & Unwin 1964)

N. McCORD, 'Aspects of the relief of poverty in early 19th century Britain', ch.4 in The long debate on poverty (I.E.A. Readings 9, 1972)

S.G. MAURICE, The Charities Act 1960 with annotations (Sweet & Maxwell 1960)

S.G. MAURICE and D.B. PARKER TUDOR – Charities (Sweet & Maxwell 1984 7th ed)

F. MIDDLETON and S. LLOYD, Charities: The new law; the Charities Act 1992 (Jordans 1992)

R.J. MORRIS, 'Voluntary societies and urban elites 1780-1850: an analysis', ch.12 in P. Borsay (ed) The Eighteenth Century Town: a reader in English urban history 1688-820 (Longman, 1990)

A.L. MORTON, A People's History of England (Lawrence and Wishart 1989)

D. OWEN, English Philanthropy 1660-1960 Harvard UP and Oxford UP 1965)

P. RIDEN, Record Sources for Local History (Batsford 1987)

M. RUBIN, Charity and Community in Medieval Cambridge (Cambridge UP 1987)

A. ROGERS, Approaches to Local History (Longman, 1977 2nd edn)

L.A. SHERIDAN and G.W. KEETON, The Modern Law of Charities (University College of Cardiff 1983)

M. SIMEY, Charity rediscovered: a study of the philanthropic effort in nineteenth-century Liverpool (1951; reprinted Liverpool UP, 1992)

P. SLACK, Poverty and Policy in Tudor and Stuart England (Longman 1988)

L. STEPHEN & S. LEE (eds), The Dictionary of National Biography (Oxford UP since 1917)

W.B. STEPHENS, Sources for English Local History (CUP 1981)

W.E. TATE, The Parish Chest (Phillimore 1983)

G.M. TREVELYAN, English Social History (Longmans, Green 1944)

R.W. UNWIN, Charity schools and the defence of Anglicanism: James Talbot, rector of Spofforth, 1700-08 (University of York Borthwick Papers, no.65)

J. WARBURTON, The Charities Act 1993. Text and Commentary (Sweet and Maxwell 1993)

INDEX

SAINT BENEDICT SCHOOL
DUFFIELD ROAD
DERBY DE22 1JD